Meet Me in Cairo

MEET ME ME IN CAIRO

Tales of Hitchin' in the '60s

JIM KERR

GRANVILLE ISLAND
PUBLISHING

ISBN: 978-1-989467-52-7 (paperback)
ISBN: 978-1-989467-65-7 (hardcover)
ISBN: 978-1-989467-53-4 (ebook)

Editor: Ed Zegarra
Copy editor: Marianne Ward
Book designer: Omar Gallegos
Maps: Jamie Fischer
Proofreader: Rebecca Coates

Granville Island Publishing Ltd.
105 – 1496 Cartwright St.
#14354, Granville Island
Vancouver, BC, Canada, V6H 4J6

604-688-0320 / 1-877-688-0320
info@granvilleislandpublishing.com
www.granvilleislandpublishing.com

Printed in Canada on recycled paper

For my mother Mary Kerr (1911–1983)

Contents

Foreword

On June 26, 1964 — in what today seems a time of innocence, peace and sanity — Kerr and his travelling buddy, Blair, left Kelowna for an unknown world that would expose them to cultures, places and peoples about which they knew nothing.

When they returned 264 days later — having taken 1,459 rides; sold their blood twice for survival money; slept in homes of distant family relations, pen pals, an orphanage, boats, jails, seedy hostels and hotels; been faced with situations that could have put them in jail (or worse), all on only $2.06 per day — neither are the same person that left home.

As a fellow globe-trotter, I can confirm that *Meet Me in Cairo* has captured this most popular rite of passage for young people of North America in the '60s: hitchhiking in Europe, Africa and the Middle East. With all the unknowns and often outrageous demands for self-reliance and resourcefulness, it was a testing ground that many had to explore. My own adventures back in the day resulted in a job in Germany — where I met my Canadian future wife of fifty-five years. What started as an opportunity to travel became an experience that unexpectedly changed me forever, just as Jim's journey did him.

In this way, *Meet Me in Cairo* is more than simply a travel book with a retrospective view of the 1960s. And, no, it's not a tale of hippiedom and free love, either — the popular media-generated image of Sixties Youth. It is a story of self-discovery and coming of age at a time when doing so in this way was a rebellion against the status quo in a Canada that was, frankly, culturally limited, leery of change and often hostile to the unconventional.

But while this is Kerr's personal story of self-reliance and identity, it is also, foremost, a colourful and often humorous narrative of what most of us back then were all about. Not sure of what we wanted — or didn't want — we simply knew we had to get away from what was leading us down a path to a place that, subconsciously, we knew we'd eventually wish had been different.

A captivating page-turner, this book is the story of two young people exploring a world of possibilities they never knew existed, finding themselves capable of exceeding the expectations they knew others had of them, and through it all uncovering meaning and potential in their own lives.

Ray Chatelin
Award-winning travel writer
Author of *The Seattle and Vancouver Book: A Complete Guide*

Introduction

I can still see the cigarette smoke in the room. It was June 1964. Blair and I had been summoned to his parents' living room to hear them tell us we were throwing our lives away. I had just told my parents I was going to drop out of university after completing just one year to hitchhike around Europe with my best friend, Blair.

At one point, it was impossible to see them through the smoke, but the message was still clear: you will be killed or your future life will be useless. My father's view was that we would both be knifed in a dark alley in southern Italy. He hated the Catholic Church, especially the Pope, and essentially all Italians, so death in Italy seemed most logical. On the other hand, he really didn't like the French either but assumed I would not die in France. As he spoke, I watched the end of his cigarette burn over the ashtray, only to be snapped up and replaced with yet another one.

Blair had just finished grade twelve and hadn't even started university. His father was in the education business and had lots of facts supporting the view that once someone dropped out of school, the chances of completing university were something like one in a million.

My mother, always wanting to be fair and not sure what tack to take, jumped on this argument. She said I would never go back to university, and all would be lost. A teacher, she told me that I would probably end up as a janitor. She must have thought this was as low as you could go, probably drawn from her teaching days. I noticed it was now becoming a contest of who was throwing their life away more. As Blair had yet to even attempt university, he was winning.

I was turning nineteen, Blair eighteen. We had grown up in a small town called Kelowna, about five hundred kilometres east of Vancouver in British Columbia. Kelowna was a perfect little town, sort of a Pleasantville. At the time, just a trip to Vancouver from Kelowna was considered a huge deal. A trip across Canada was an adventure that few had taken. And a trip to Europe alone and not on a bus tour? Well, no one had ever thought of that.

After a horrendous first year at university in Vancouver I needed to escape. What could be better than to see the world with my best buddy? Our plan was to hitchhike from Kelowna to New York and take a student ship to England. From there, we would hitchhike around Europe and, hopefully, farther afield, and return the next year by plane to New York. With little money, we planned to live on about two dollars a day.

• • •

Following my mother's death, some seventeen years after our meeting at Blair's parents' home, I was going through her things and found a photo album I had never seen. Inside were all the letters, twenty-four of them, I had written to her on our trip.

She had preserved each one in a separate plastic folder, together with its envelope and stamps. On the top of each letter, she had written the date when she had received it. She must have read each one time and time again. Of course, the letters were an edited version of what we were actually doing, but I had spent hours on them, making sure my mother would not worry.

Reading them in my late thirties, I understood a lot more about that meeting at Blair's parents' house. My mother had been so proud of me, an only child, going to university — considered a status symbol by her friends. However, the status symbol was flying the coop, and worse, my mother's closest friends all had perfect children attending the University of British Columbia. Having me throw this all away must have shattered her dreams. At the time, I had anticipated my parents' objections but felt it was just the typical parental reaction when a son proposed something radically different. Now, I realized that it must have been a devastating blow.

Many decades later, in my seventies, I stumbled again upon this same book of letters, along with part of my old diary and a few pictures of our trip. Blair also sent me a diary that he had kept, as well as a picture or two.

Prompted by this rediscovery, I decided to write our story. A tale of two naive young men who came of age through hitchhiking across North America, Europe, North Africa and the Middle East. Both left Kelowna, travelled on fumes and came back alive to complete their studies at university and go on to have extraordinarily normal lives.

This is that book.

1

Messed Up

Twenty years from now you will be more disappointed by the things you didn't do than by the ones you did do. So, throw off the bow-lines, sail away from the safe harbour.

— attributed to Mark Twain

At age eighteen I was failing university and majoring in bridge. It was 1964. To say I was messed up was an understatement. I had grown up in the small town of Kelowna, a great place to spend a childhood: safe and middle-class. Comfortable but sheltered, it was the most homogenous town you could ever find. There was no ethnic diversity, no people of colour and very few non-Christians. No one was wealthy or really poor. It was the type of town where everyone waited to cross the street at one of the few traffic lights despite not a car in sight. Jaywalking was out of the question. One's view of the world was severely limited. It wasn't until I attended first-year university that I even heard of someone who was Jewish.

Like all my friends, I went to the University of British Columbia after grade twelve. I was hopeless in the arts so enrolled in pre-engineering, a career that my father always wanted. But soon I realized that engineering and Jim were not a good fit.

Somehow, I had missed the fact that engineering required some practical mechanical skills. I had none. I was probably the least mechanically inclined person in the world.

At the start of my second term in early January, I started playing bridge all night in a large student residence. At three in the morning, when someone dropped out of a game, everyone knew that all you had to do was knock on my door and I would jump out of bed and go downstairs for a few hands. Soon, I was missing every breakfast. The earliest class I made started at one o'clock in the afternoon. My marks were crashing.

Almost every second day, I had been writing my high school girlfriend, but by February her letters stopped coming. For some bizarre reason, she thought I might not be the success she had hoped for and dumped me as a loser. I was going nowhere fast. By March, I made the obvious decision that engineering was not for me.

I needed a drastic change.

• • •

I loved to hitchhike. I had first started hitchhiking short distances at age sixteen with my buddy Blair. We had been hitchhiking out of Kelowna for years and loved it. On countless weekends, we thumbed our way to Vancouver, Seattle or whatever location caught our eye. We came to consider ourselves masters at the game.

I first met Blair when he sat down beside me in the second row of our high school dance band. He had just moved to Kelowna, and we both played the saxophone. Even though Blair was enrolled in a grade behind me, we hit it off immediately in that first chance meeting. More outgoing, confident and positive than I, he was in a way a foil to my shy personality.

Despite our natural and easy friendship, we were quite different. I was totally into sports, participating in everything, including track and field, while Blair didn't participate in sports at all. Academically, my best subjects were math and then math again, while Blair excelled in English and French — my worst subjects (I only got through French when a buddy found the exact grade 12 French exam to be given the next day and shared it with me). We would talk constantly during band practice, and it was inevitable that we started to hang out with each other after school. We soon found out that we both shared a taste for adventure and travel within British Columbia.

My first after-school encounters with Blair were to drive in his father's old, dilapidated Nash to dances in the town of Penticton, some thirty miles away. (Canada didn't switch to the metric system till the mid-seventies, so all distances in Canada are shown in miles.) I was a disaster when it came to asking girls to dance at our local dances, whereas Blair had all the confidence in the world and never feared rejection. One night I came up with the idea of simply changing the location of the dance to another city where the girls did not know me. Out of town I changed personalities and lost my fear of rejection, knowing there were no consequences. Voila! We were off and running. Though we would usually 'strike out' at these dances, we really enjoyed each other's company and talked non-stop on the long drives to and from each dance.

The real click happened when we both wanted to expand our horizons and spend the weekends in the big city, Vancouver, some three hundred miles to the west. I was able to borrow my father's car and made up a story that we would spend the weekend with our imaginary friend in Vernon, just thirty miles away. Instead, we would drive all the way to Vancouver and back over two days, sleeping in the car. To not arouse suspicion,

Blair had figured out how to disconnect the mileage meter and reengage it about one hundred miles from home, to make it look like we had driven to Vernon and back instead of the approximately seven hundred miles we had actually driven.

Soon we discovered that we both loved hitchhiking. Being on the road more regularly freed up my personality even more. Not knowing what would happen next, and knowing I would never see the driver again, I was far more open than normal. Easing my transition, Blair would often dominate the discussions with our drivers while I sat back and listened. Several weekends we would just put our thumbs out and hitch all the way to Vancouver, not knowing where we would sleep or when we would hitch back the next day.

• • •

I had read a few books on travelling around Europe, which seemed like a great spot to start my escape. Why Europe? Who knows? It seemed distant and exotic. I would drop out of university and hitchhike around the continent. Maybe when I came back I would have a few ideas of what to do with my life.

Not too keen on going by myself, I wrote a long letter to Blair, who was still in Kelowna, asking him to join me on an adventure of a lifetime and hitch around Europe. He was just finishing up grade twelve and enjoying life and had no pressing need to escape to the unknown. Thus, I was surprised when Blair wrote back that he was in and would love to go.

Later, I learned that he had plastered the walls and ceilings of his bedroom with pictures of German cities like Bonn and Stuttgart. Why Germany? I had no idea, but staring at those posters every night had made him wonder what those towns really looked like. Coincidentally, those images had instilled in

Blair a desire to go to Europe too. The timing of my letter was perfect.

But there was one problem: he had no money, nor did I. Therefore, we would work in Kelowna for the early part of the summer, saving all we could, then perhaps do some work in Europe if we needed more funds. I was able to start work two months earlier than Blair, since he was stuck in high school, but he could use the money he had saved for university. We would hitch everywhere. It was perfect. No longer did I feel like the biggest loser. I had a goal to embark on an adventure that no one else, it seemed to me, had even considered. For once, the future looked bright.

There was an additional issue: my marks. Should I just blow the year and then come back and do first year over again, or pull a rabbit out of a hat and try to pass all my courses so I would get full credit for a year of university? I chose the second alternative, worked very hard for a few weeks and squeaked through, passing all my courses.

By then I had become so comfortable hitchhiking that I hitched straight back to Kelowna from Vancouver only an hour after my last exam. I even bet someone who was leaving for Kelowna an hour after me that I could beat them home hitching. I won.

I quickly got a job working for the City of Kelowna, a union job that paid a fortune. Although it officially consisted of maintaining the city's streets, it was mostly standing around holding a shovel and hoping not to be seen by the good tax-paying citizens of Kelowna. But within the first week of being home, my travel plans hit a snag. Blair told me he had changed his mind and was no longer going. He thought it would be better to finish university first, then travel the world. Of course, he was right, but I was one messed-up guy with no future at all. Finishing university now was simply not an option for me. We spent a week going back and forth about Blair going or not going. My most persuasive argument was that students who dropped out intending to go to university later were born losers, and Blair was not a loser. Eventually, he caved. He was in and wouldn't change his mind again. He knew in his heart he would go on to university after we returned. "Let's just go," I told him.

Another problem? Neither of us could point out to our parents anyone from Kelowna who had gone to Europe, other than a few over-fifty-year-olds who had taken bus tours of England or France. Who knew what evils lurked in dark alleys in the depths of Europe? If you were brought up in Kelowna, the world started and ended in Kelowna.

Blair and I bought some maps of Canada, the eastern US and Europe and sat down every night to plan our trip. We knew we would hitchhike across Canada, then down to the US to see Washington, DC, and New York. Then, we would see England for a while and head over to the continent of Europe to see the major capitals. Once in Europe, we would see what grabbed us and go from there.

I had heard of a student ship that left New York for England on July 28, 1964, and decided to get tickets. Apparently, the ship often carried back to Europe European university students who had taken a year to study in the US. What really appealed to us was the cost: about half the price of a regular cruise line crossing the Atlantic. To return, we bought an open, one-way ticket for the following year with Icelandic Airlines, the cheapest airline flying to and from Europe and also the slowest. It left from Luxembourg, stopped in Iceland and landed in New York a day later. With these two major expenditures out of the way, it was only a case of saving all we could and leaving Kelowna in time to make the departure date for our ship in New York.

Our goal was to leave around July 1, 1964, hitch across Canada, see some of the US and catch our ship in New York on July 28. We hoped to have about four hundred dollars each. Living on two dollars a day, that would allow us to travel about two hundred days, which was 60 percent less than the famous travel book at the time, *Europe on 5 Dollars a Day*.

As our departure date drew nearer, our plans kept changing and the pressure from our parents to abort increased. About two weeks before departure we decided that the wait was killing us, so we moved up our plans by a week. If I worked to my next payday, I would have almost exactly the same amount of money that Blair had saved for university but was now using for our trip. Just finishing his exams, he had hoped to work for a week to top up his funds but was now out of time. We were closer to $380 than the expected $400, but it seemed more important to leave before something prevented us from going.

With only a few days to get ready, there was lots to do. The most important item was our backpack. We took our old canvas Boy Scout packs. They were heavy and ugly but indestructible, with a wooden frame, and large enough to easily hold everything we owned. If the pack got wet, it would add at least five pounds, since canvas soaks up water. But they were the only ones we had.

Blair plastered the outside of his pack with a few Canadian flags, since we understood that the 'ugly American' view of tourists was starting to surface in Europe. He found a great flag that covered the front of his pack. We wanted everyone to know we were pure Canadians and thought it might help in hitchhiking if drivers saw the red-and-white Canadian flag on our pack.

We took sleeping bags, jeans, rain jackets, spare shoes and most of the clothes we owned. Both sleeping bags were good for temperatures above 70 degrees Fahrenheit, meaning they were useless. They wouldn't keep us warm at all, but that seemed irrelevant since we hoped to sleep in some sort of warm building each night, not outdoors. Because we both had few clothes to our name, it was tough to overpack.

I had read of pickpockets and of travellers losing all their money. If this happened to us, our trip would be over. We decided to use travellers' cheques. If stolen, we could go to the nearest American Express office, give them the serial numbers and get the exact number of cheques back within an hour. We each had our passport, birth certificate, driver's licence and for Blair, a picture of his girlfriend. I had burned mine.

My father was very fond of Crown Royal rye whiskey. Each bottle came in a soft purple bag that closed with a gold tassel. He had them all over the house. These bags were perfect to hold my money, travellers' cheques, passports and other things that might be important to both of us. My plan was to take the Crown Royal bag and stuff it into the crotch of my pants, then tie the tassel to my belt loop. Blair did the same thing with his pants but used a cloth bag instead. It would be a bit awkward when asked for ID or money, because we would have to reach into our crotch, but it would also be very difficult for a pickpocket to get in there and steal our funds.

2

Pen Pals

The world is a book, and those who do not travel read only a page.

— *Saint Augustine*

My father was a Rotarian, part of a worldwide organization called Rotary International. In Kelowna, Rotarians were a group of older men who met monthly for lunch in formal wear, meaning a sports jacket and a tie. It was a club restricted to those who owned a business or worked in one of the white-collar professions and tried to do good deeds for the city and county. Each month, my father would get the Rotarian magazine delivered to our home.

When I was about sixteen, I noticed a section in the back of the publication that listed younger people who wanted to be pen pals, mainly from the US. I thought I would give it a shot. I wrote a girl the same age as me who lived in southern California, asking to be her pen pal, and we exchanged letters for a year. I imagined her as some nubile nymph and described myself as a part-time bodybuilder who was captain of all our high school sports teams, and of course, first in my class.

I had been going to the Kelowna Public Library every few days to get books on travelling in Europe, including the famous book mentioned earlier, *Europe on 5 Dollars a Day* by Arthur Frommer. Written in the late 1950s, this was the first book that revolutionized travel for young people on a limited budget. Until then, most travel was on bus tours by those close to retirement. The book outlined how to find youth hostels and save money on food, restaurants and transportation. Of course, five dollars a day was a fortune to Blair and me, but it was a step in the right direction. While talking to the librarian, who had been to Europe, I mentioned that five dollars a day was way out of our league. She was very helpful and suggested ways of cutting down our costs, including staying with relatives.

"It's too bad you don't have any pen pals in Europe," she said, out of the blue.

I leapt on her comment, rushing back home to look at all those old Rotary magazines to see if anyone who lived in Europe was looking for a pen pal. My thought was that we could get free accommodation and meals. Unfortunately, there were no European addresses.

My new librarian friend piped up: "I've heard that if you address a letter to 'The Newspaper' in any city in Europe, your letter will get to one of the larger newspapers in that city and they might publish your ad for a pen pal." It seemed like a long shot, but why not try it?

The plan was to write to The Newspaper in ten large cities in Europe with an ad from me, which started with something like "Wonderful university student from Canada looking for a pen pal in [insert name of city]."

I kept the ad short, hoping for a better chance to be published. My ad was in English, since I had no clue how to translate it. Besides, it would be far better if whoever answered the ad spoke fluent English.

If I got a reply, I would write back immediately, saying I thought they were wonderful and was so pleased to hear from them. Then, if by chance they replied to that letter, in my second letter I would say something like, "Guess what? Last night I decided to go to Europe with my best friend, and I'm wondering by chance if we would be able to see you," meaning, "Can you put us up for a night or two?"

Blair and I spent a night choosing ten cities to write to, like London, Paris, Edinburgh, Glasgow (we were both of Scottish ancestry), Athens, Berlin, Gothenburg and Stockholm. (We had heard the girls in Sweden were all blonde and beautiful.) We divided the cities in two, with Blair and I each sending off pen pal requests to five of them.

A week later, believe it or not, we started getting replies. It was working. For some reason, we had used my parents' address for both my letters and Blair's. Replies came in first from London. One of the first days, my parents received over a hundred letters, all from prospective pen pals in that great city. I couldn't believe it. I found out that my letter to The Newspaper had been directed to *The Times* in London. Someone at *The Times* had found my request intriguing and had put my small ad for pen pals on the front page of their second section. We got so many replies that the next day the head of the Kelowna post office visited my parents and accused them of running some sort of mail scam. The officials demanded an explanation and wanted to shut down the scam immediately.

Soon we started getting letters from Berlin, Athens, Glasgow and Gothenburg in Sweden. Blair and I had a lot of fun replying to these letters. Each night, we got all the letters we received, mostly from London, and put all the replies from males in the wastepaper basket. Some letters were from women much older than us (as old as thirty-five!), many from London. I guess I had forgotten to stress that we were hoping to receive a reply from someone our own age. These invitations did sound intriguing, to use a word, since neither of us had ever gone out with an older woman and were certain we were missing something. In the end, we restricted our replies to those in our own age group. We picked the ten best letters from girls from London and sent an initial reply, hoping to get back a few responses quickly. We were hoping to find four pen pals who lived in London, who would put us up for two nights each.

When it looked like the letters would never stop, and we had more than two hundred replies, we became pickier and pickier. One evening, while opening the letters, Blair started yelling.

"Jim, Jim, Jim — look at this! I can't believe it." He was holding something up that I couldn't see. "It's a picture that was in this envelope from Athens. She looks like a model. Here's another picture of her and her best friend. Jesus."

Blair passed the pictures to me. He was right. Both women looked gorgeous.

He went on, as excited as ever. "It says here they are both part-time models and really would like to be my pen pal. They loved the ad."

Blair grabbed the other ten letters from Athens and without opening them, stuffed them into the wastepaper basket. He started drafting a reply, thinking the models might disappear if he didn't get back to them that evening.

We did not receive any replies from Stockholm or Paris, which was very disappointing. We could only assume that some of our original letters to 'The Newspaper' were not published. Not all the letters were from fair damsels. From Glasgow and Edinburgh, we chose a few guys.

In the end, Blair and I heard back from prospective pen pals in six cities in Europe. We marked each of those cities on our map, as well as the location of a number of long-lost relatives in England so we could figure out a hitching route at minimum cost and hopefully live off our newfound friends, our pen pals.

BRITISH
COLUMBIA

ALBERTA

SASKATCHEWAN

MANITOBA

Kelowna
Start
End
Cranbrook

Calgary

Winnipeg

WASHINGTON

UNITED STATES OF AMERICA   CANADA

OREGON

IDAHO

MONTANA

NORTH DAKOTA

MINNE

SOUTH DAKOTA

WYOMING

NEBRASKA

UTAH

Mode of Travel

Hitchhiking
Boat
Plane

North America

The map shows our hitchhiking route in the summer of 1964, from our start in Kelowna, BC, via the Trans-Canada Highway to Montreal and on to New York City. From New York we took a student ship to England. We returned by plane to New York in the spring of '65. Our hitchhiking route started directly from the airport, crossing the USA in just four days to a small fork in the road in Idaho. I took the left fork to the town of Kelowna and Blair the right fork to Cranbrook.

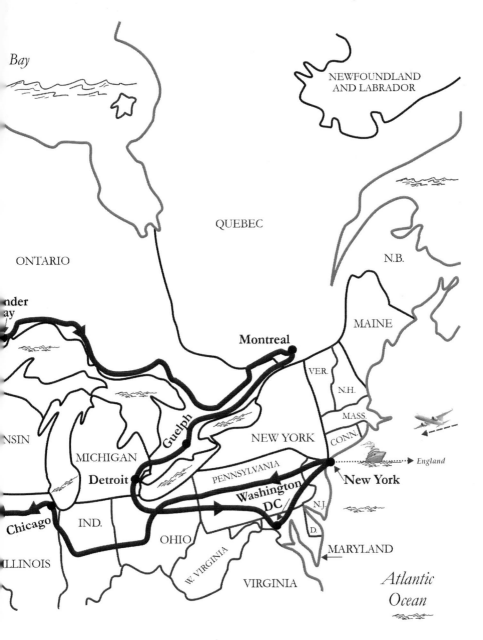

3

Help Us To Europe

Hitchhiking was such a pure form of existence. You'd wake up in the morning, and you'd have no idea what your next day was going to be. And that's something I've never been able to shake.

— *John Hawkes*

I didn't sleep the night before Blair and I were to leave. I must have gone over my list of what to take a million times, knowing there was no going back. Better to take more and mail it back than less, I figured. Late at night, with only a few hours to go, I thought we needed a hitching sign of some sort. With something catchy written on it. After many attempts, I finally came up with the phrase "Help Us To Europe," which might make some drivers curious enough to stop and pick us up.

We had experimented with signs before while hitchhiking in Canada, and none had worked. The downside was that if you were hitching to, say, Vancouver from Kelowna and your sign said "Vancouver," only those going to Vancouver would pick you up. You would miss all those rides going, say, a third of the way. For that reason, Blair and I had scrapped using signs early on in our hitchhiking career. However, "Help Us To Europe" had a different ring to it. In this case, our objective was to get rides from drivers who had been to Europe or were curious about whether we really were going to Europe. I thought it gave a safe message as well.

To create my artistic masterpiece, I went to my parents' basement and found a can of red paint and a small paintbrush. Upstairs, I found a piece of white cardboard about three feet by three feet, the perfect size for a sign. I took my time and painted the letters using a bright red paint in bold print. It turned out great and, most importantly, was readable from a distance.

A second idea, which came to me later that night around five in the morning was to grab one of the ugly suitcases stored away that my family never used, go down to our kitchen, and load it up with every canned food item I thought would last. I looked in every cupboard, finding canned hams, tuna, etc., and jammed them all into the small suitcase. It must have weighed over thirty pounds. This way, Blair and I could open, say, a canned ham on the side of the Trans-Canada Highway and eat like kings without spending a cent. I even remembered to borrow a can opener.

At last it was daybreak and time to depart. Opposing my travel plans to the bitter end, my parents refused to take me to our starting point, which was just at the outskirts of Kelowna. But in the end, they changed their minds. They decided to drop me off and not stay long, which I appreciated more than they knew. Blair's parents had come to the same conclusion and dropped him off but didn't stay long either. The goodbyes to my mother were as hard for me as they were for her. She was still hoping I would change my mind. As each day had passed before our departure, she had become sadder and sadder. Blair's girlfriend, Cheryl, did see us off and stayed with us for a while, taking a picture of us hitching for our first ride.

The picture on the right really captures the differences in our personalities at the time: Blair on the left, confident and looking directly at the camera; me on the right, looking nerd-like, head down, with one arm behind my back, staring at the pavement rather than the camera.

Ready to catch our first ride just on the edge of Kelowna. Dressed in our finest, before jeans became fashionable. The words "Help Us To Europe" are clearly visible on the freshly painted sign in front of the proud artist, your author.

For our place of departure, Blair and I had chosen a spot about a half-mile out of Kelowna, right across from the local shopping centre, Shops Capri. We were on the main highway north, which after about forty miles, met up with a highway that would take us to the Trans-Canada Highway. From there, it was a short 2,800-mile hitchhike to Montreal, our first destination. We hardly had time to set up our sign in front of us and get our smiles working when a brand new Mercedes stopped to pick us up with a young couple inside. We couldn't believe it. Our wait was less than ten minutes. Perhaps the sign was going to work.

I had a grin from ear to ear as Blair and I sat in the back seat of that Mercedes, my new sign between us. We were doing it. We had no idea when we were coming back. Time meant nothing. We did have a plane ticket coming back, but that was open for a year. Our trip had no ending.

Travelling without a deadline, we were free, on an adventure of a lifetime, with no fear. Our only goal was to keep travelling, as nothing else really mattered. I have rarely been as happy as I was in that first half hour, with the whole world in front of me. We were on our way, and where we ended up that night or the next really didn't matter.

"Are you guys really going to Europe, and where have you been so far?" was the first question our driver asked. Blair jumped in and explained that this was our first ride.

"We're hitching to my uncle's in Montreal and then heading to New York to catch a ship to Europe next month. Have you been there? What's it like?"

Our driver then went over all the places in Europe he had been to, telling us in no uncertain terms that France was the best by far and backing it up with example after example. We soaked it all in. As he went on, though, I noticed we were already at a fork in the road where we needed to get off, as our driver was heading north and we were heading east toward Montreal.

"Stop, please, we need to get out here," I said, interrupting his story on Paris. He jammed on the brakes and came to a full stop just past the intersection.

We thanked our driver and his wife a million times, and Blair went back to get our packs and the suitcase of food out of the trunk of the car. I went to grab my new sign, but it would not come off the back seat. It was stuck. In an instant, I realized what I had done. The red paint was still wet, and in the hour that the sign had been resting against the seat, it had stuck firmly to it. Slowly, I peeled the sign off their luxurious leather seat, hearing a half-scraping, half-squealing sound, and looked in horror at the words in bright red now clearly visible on the seat in reverse:

ƧU ꟼ⅃ƎH
OT
ƎꟼOЯUƎ

Oh God! I grabbed my sign and quickly jumped out of the car. Luckily, the couple had been chatting with Blair, giving him last-minute advice as he stood by their window with our packs, and they had not heard a thing. I quickly thanked the couple again and turned toward the side of the road. As soon as their car was out of sight, I screamed at Blair, "Run for the woods — now!"

As we ran, I told Blair how I had screwed up. We ran far into the woods and got down behind some trees, out of sight, to wait until we thought the coast was clear.

They were not coming back for us.

After twenty minutes of hiding in the woods, Blair and I continued on foot through the forest back to the highway, which soon fed into the Trans-Canada Highway, Canada's main transcontinental artery.

This was the first of a number of incidents on the trip that I would come to regret. I know we should have pointed out to the nice couple that gave us our first ride that I had accidently ruined their back seat. But I knew the consequences would have probably meant reimbursing them for the cost of cleaning the paint off the seat, if it could be done at all. We would break our budget after only one hour of our trip. I chose to keep our money and continue on instead of doing the right thing. It might be a tad late, but if the driver or his wife is reading this, or their children have heard the story, please get ahold of me. I will gladly pay for the damage now, plus a bit of interest.

We were heading for Montreal, where the first of many free places to stay awaited us. This time it was Blair's uncle's home. We had written a week earlier telling his uncle that we would expect to make the trip in about seven days.

We put out our thumbs and rearranged the still-legible sign in front of us. In less than twenty minutes, we caught another ride. Not a Mercedes, but it was a ride. The sign was really working.

That first day, Blair and I were so wired that we hitched all night and into the next day. We were getting rides very quickly, even late at night. Each time we got picked up, I would ask the driver why he picked us up, and the number one reason given was the sign. Many didn't believe we were going to Europe but picked us up anyway.

"So, you're not really going to Europe, are you guys?" was often the first thing that came out of a new driver's mouth. "It got me to stop to pick you up, though, as I wanted to know. I have always wanted to go there. My dad fought there in the war in Europe, you know — he hated it."

Another driver gave us a lecture. "You know, kids, there's an ocean called the Atlantic between Canada and Europe." He slowly explained the geography, to make sure we could follow his profound knowledge of the country. "I hate to tell you this, but you're not gonna be able to hitch all the way to Europe like your sign says, because of this ocean. I thought you should know this now because once you get to the end of Canada, you're going to be very disappointed."

What do you say? We stayed silent and thanked him for his brilliant observation.

We came across a few drivers who had lived in Europe and wanted to see if we were going to their country. The answer of course was always "Yes, we are." Then the driver would talk non-stop about why theirs was the best country in Europe.

The author clearly demonstrating how to get a ride on the Trans-Canada Highway.

After hitching for thirty-six hours straight, with little sleep other than what we could grab in the back seat of a ride, we saw a government campsite on the side of the road and asked our driver to stop and let us off. It was somewhere in the middle of the Canadian prairies. We found a campsite and set up our sleeping bags on the ground. We had no tent, of course, but we were long on food. We had made our best effort to barely open the suitcase of canned goods until now, but we were starved, so we feasted on cold canned soup, a canned ham, and a can of tuna. We crawled into our sleeping bags, which kept us barely warm in the 70 degrees Fahrenheit evening weather, and fell right to sleep. We slept forever and it was late in the morning when we finally awoke. From this point, we slept in government campsites along the way to Montreal and prayed it wouldn't rain as we slept in the open.

Three days later we would reach Montreal.

4

The Art of Hitchhiking

Alice asked the Cheshire Cat, who was sitting in a tree,
"What road do I take?"
The cat said, "Where do you want to go?"
"I don't know," Alice answered.
"Then," said the cat, "It really doesn't matter, does it?"

— *paraphrased from Alice's Adventures*
in Wonderland, Lewis Carroll

A few years earlier, we had just stuck out our thumbs and hoped to get a ride. By now we had enough experience to be able to understand why we would get rides quickly on some occasions and on others wind up stuck on the side of a highway for hours. The more tricks and tips we learned, the less time we stood at the side of the road waiting to be picked up.

First, there was our appearance. When we were about seventeen, I can recall a big argument with Blair over what to wear when hitchhiking. Most drivers have a fear of the unknown, and picking up two rough-looking characters with their thumbs out isn't going to fit the bill. We became obsessed with looking and dressing our best in the hope that this would entice a driver to stop.

On one occasion, at Blair's insistence, we dressed up in white shirts with ties for a long hitchhike from Kelowna to Seattle, a distance of four hundred miles. We were trying to look like the clean-cut, church-attending, all-American poster boy. However, it didn't seem to make any difference. The perfect balance was to look clean-cut but not go so far as to look like a missionary. We axed the very-well-dressed-kid routine after just one try.

In any case, if we waited on the side of the road with our thumbs in the air long enough, a driver would eventually stop and pick us up. Sometimes it was just five minutes, other times it could be the entire day. To increase our odds of being picked up quickly, we stood tall, looked like naive kids from a small town (which we were), and above all made eye contact with the driver.

An early lesson: location, location, location.

Even Cher, dressed as only Cher could be, would not get a ride if she were standing right after a blind corner with nowhere for a car to stop. It would simply be too dangerous for a driver to pull over. Where someone stands on the side of the road to hitchhike is the biggest factor in getting a ride quickly. We began keeping an eye out for a safe edge of road just behind us, so a driver could easily pull over and not hold up traffic. A hitchhiker wants the driver to easily see a stopping point, say fifty yards past where they are standing. In the dark, good spots are lit areas, such as just past a gas station. Generally, we were too chicken to ask drivers for rides at gas stations, but a wimpy face under the streetlamp only twenty yards past the gas station worked wonders.

When drivers passed by slowly, we could easily make eye contact. Of course, most of them just kept going and often accelerated past us. On these occasions Blair and I would have a contest to dream up the most original swear word to apply to a driver who dared not pick us up.

Blair demonstrating where not to hitchhike.

Junctions were always a good place to hitch from. Even without a stop sign, most drivers will slow down in case a car is coming from the other direction. Our approach was to stand just past the junction, with smiles on our cute-as-can-be faces, and try to make eye contact.

Heavy, large packs are an issue for the distance hitchhiker, though, especially if it is raining and they become soaking wet. We decided early on to hide one of our packs in a ditch at the side of the road so that a driver would just see a single pack, with a Canadian flag prominently displayed. Our worry was that a driver might drive on if they thought there was no room for two packs in their car. There was always room, though. Once they stopped for one pack, it was just a matter of proper packing to jam both packs in.

A potentially disastrous pitfall in hitchhiking is to get dropped off on the outskirts leading into a large city. No one picks up a hitchhiker when they are heading for the centre of a city. If this happened, we just gave up and walked to the downtown core, then hopefully got a ride out in our direction. To avoid this problem, we would ask where the driver was going. If he told us he was just going to the outskirts of a large city, we would ask him to drop us off in a town before the city, even though it was farther from our destination. Often when we explained the issue, the driver would take us to the other end of town, or at least the centre.

It was usually when we waited longer than usual that Blair and I would field test different strategies. If Blair was looking particularly haggard one morning and putting drivers off, I would stand in front of him, shielding him from a potential driver's sight. Another strategy would be to use a windmill movement with our right arm: we each circled our whole arm, clockwise, with our thumbs out. It looked quite impressive when we choreographed it together.

We devised a strategy to prevent a driver from changing their mind once they'd stopped. One of us would immediately run, not walk, up to the driver's side without a backpack and thank him "so much" for stopping. The other would then grab both packs and approach the back door opposite the driver. Most of the time it was unlocked, so the next move was to open the door and get the packs ready to shove in the car. Whoever was at the driver's window would ask him where he was going. Probably 99 percent of the time, we would say, "That's great. That's where we're going too," even if we didn't have a clue where they were heading. Since it had to be at least a mile down the road, we'd usually just take a chance and run with it. Rarely would we refuse a ride. But if we saw an open bottle of rye on the front seat, or the driver leered at us, we shook our heads and refused the ride.

The job of the guy in the front seat was to get the driver talking, and most of them loved to talk. Most guys who picked us up were lonely, had a long drive ahead of them and wanted company. We would learn about their love life, why they hated their job and often, the politics of the region or country. Each driver gave us a different perspective on the country's issues and problems. Often, the next driver would have the exact opposite view on the same issue. For example, on the Prairies a lot of drivers were resentful of those that lived in BC, like us, thinking we were all lazy part-time communists. Common ground was found on the issue of Quebec, though. Almost everyone thought Quebec should never be part of Canada. In Ontario, the drivers all thought the West was crazy and that Ontario was the economic engine that drove all of Canada. It seemed the best parts of Canada were those places within fifty miles of where our drivers lived.

With hitchhiking one enters a new world with every ride. It's the road that determines the route, and where one ends up at night is never certain. Hitching is really an attitude toward travel as much as it is getting from one point to another. Unless one really has to get to somewhere, the destination is secondary. For example, travelling by train means one knows exactly where and when they will arrive. It's always certain. If one meets anyone, it's often a fellow traveller in similar circumstances and little is learned about the people in the country visible through the window of the train. On arrival, one might walk around and see a few pretty buildings, and that's it. On to another city.

One might get sidetracked by a driver's hospitality and be invited to dinner and into their home instead of one's intended destination. It is free-flowing, flexible, liberating. It's that freedom on the road, never really knowing what will happen next, that makes hitchhiking superior in a way to other forms of travelling. Of course, embracing the unexpected comes with its fair share of bad times, like really bad times when it's raining. It will be wet, getting dark, and not a car is stopping. But eventually someone stops. And with the next ride, one forgets all that. Once again, all is wonderful.

5

The Odd Job

. . . "What if I fall?"
"Oh, but my darling,
What if you fly?"

— Erin Hanson

We made very good time and knocked on the door of Blair's uncle's home two days earlier than expected. Blair's uncle lived just north of Montreal, in the town of Laval, in the middle of a subdivision. To us it was heaven, but in reality, it was a small home set in the suburbs. I could have imagined Norman Rockwell living next door. Despite arriving far sooner than expected, we were welcomed warmly and invited to spread out over their basement spare room. Our first showers in days were so great that we must have drained all their hot water. The trip from Kelowna to Montreal had not only been faster than expected, but cheaper. I sent a postcard back to my parents. It started off with the line "Well, I made it all the way to Montreal in five days and spent only eleven cents so far. That's around two cents a day, Mom, way under budget."

Since we were ahead of schedule, and our student ship didn't leave New York for another two and a half weeks, we made the call to stay with Blair's uncle for about a week or more, rather than the four or five days we planned.

Since we had time to burn, we decided it was time to earn some money and started looking at want ads for jobs that could help us add to our war chest. One problem: most people who lived in Montreal spoke French, and my French was hopeless; therefore, any job that involved French, like being a waiter, was a no-go. Blair, on the other hand, wasn't at all bad at French, but not quite good enough to work in the language.

That night, we scoured the want ads in the *Montreal Gazette* and found, of all things, an ad to sell subscriptions to their own newspaper. No experience needed. We liked those words. Just show up. We hitched down to their office, only to be shown to a dark, dismal boiler room with no windows and lots of small desks separated from one another by cardboard walls. The designated subscriptions-sales desk had just a phone and a list of phone numbers on it, but above on the wall loomed four-foot-high boards on three sides, all covered in large print with a flowchart of answers to our prospective buyers' questions.

We each received a sheet of phone numbers that belonged to English-speaking families. All we had to do was follow the plan above us on the cardboard wall that surrounded our little desk, and we would get two dollars for each *Montreal Gazette* subscription we sold. On our trip, two bucks was a lot of money.

In front of us, at the top of the cardboard sheet, was our opening line, when and if we got someone on the phone. It said, "How would you like to help your neighbourhood paper boy earn a fifty-dollar Canada Savings Bond to use toward his higher education?"

How could anyone say no to this question? That was the whole idea. We were to start each call with this question, no exceptions. However, after the first question, things got a little complicated if someone actually responded. The maze of answers above us anticipated each reply to our opening line from our victims. We just needed to find our own reply quickly on the cardboard above us and read it out to our potential buyer in time. Sometimes it took a full five seconds for us to find the exact response.

For example, if they said in very broken English, "We only speak French, so why would I need an English newspaper?" I would find the response to that excuse somewhere on the panel above me and read out very slowly, "All the better for you to learn English by reading an English paper. Each day you get another English lesson."

After two hours and thirty calls, I had sold nothing. Blair was not doing any better, but suddenly, he got a fish on the line and actually sold a subscription. Two bucks for Blair. Two hours later, I was still zero for fifty calls. Blair's luck didn't continue. It was time to give this up and collect our two bucks.

Of course, the fellow running the place said we couldn't get the two bucks now, as the subscription had to be verified, but by late the next day, he would have the money ready. To us, two bucks was two bucks, so we showed up late the next day, after hitching downtown, and collected our two dollars. I coerced Blair into buying me a beer with his newfound wealth.

That night, we found another potential money-maker, selling *Encyclopedia Britannica* volumes door to door. All we had to do was report to a downtown address. If we managed to sell even one subscription, there were huge commissions available to us (at least twenty dollars per set). Blair and I agreed to split the money if either of us was lucky enough to actually sell something.

We hitched to their office and were then taken by van to a lower-middle-class area, where we were told to read the selling kit. What we were really selling was a chance for poor families to give their children a head start, subscribing to a series of encyclopedias that would be delivered every few weeks or so. The cost was nothing to start, but unfortunately, the bill went on and on for many years, until the poor subscriber gave up the payments and stopped getting the books. They really preyed on the poor, who had a goal of getting their children a good education. The racket was to sell these parents on the idea that subscribing to the *Encyclopedia* was the best way to do this.

Blair and I started down the street, me taking one side and he the other, eager to see who could get the first sale. When I knocked on my first door, the flaw was apparent right away. The homeowner didn't have a clue what I was saying and told me in French to get the hell off the property. Blair had the same response. As we worked our way down the street, we realized we had been dropped into a French area of Montreal. There was no hope. Besides, I was not happy selling these costly books to unsuspecting poor families. Again, it was time to abandon ship. Before we could even complete one block of homes, we were hitching back to Blair's uncle's home, ready to try something else.

That afternoon, we found a new prospective job that would not require any interactions with the French-speaking inhabitants of Montreal: worm-picking.

The idea was that we would go out onto some field at night with lights, just pick worms off the grass and get paid large sums of money for it. We were to meet at some street corner five miles away, then be taken to an area where we would pick worms. What could go wrong?

After phoning and being accepted, Blair and I were told to meet our new employer, who would be sitting in a truck on a street corner about ten miles from where we were staying. That should have been a hint. We went ahead anyway and met the fellow who was running the worm-picking gig, plus a number of other people who seemed a lot like ourselves: young, naive and poorly dressed. He explained that we would wear a helmet with a big light on the front, just like a miner's. We each received a bucket and pair of plastic gloves. The plan was for ten of us to go out in complete darkness and find a worm, attracted by our light, and put it in the bucket. Simple. We would be paid once we filled our bucket with worms.

In the dead of night, we were driven in the back of the man's truck out to the edge of what looked like a golf course and let out to grab some worms. The problem was that the worms were on the ground, and I was far above it. When I finally found one and grabbed it, the worm would split in half and I would end up with only half of one in my bucket. We were not good at this. I estimated that by the time I filled one bucket with worms, it would be noon the next day. To make things worse, I noticed that the guy in charge was not watching us but pacing around, chain-smoking and looking in the direction of the clubhouse and other roads leading in our direction.

Soon, a security car drove up. After a quick conversation between our boss and a guard, we were told to get in the truck because we were off to another location with better worms. I realized the obvious: our employer had no permission to pick worms on the golf course. The company was only using this location until we were caught, and would just keep doing this routine all night. Blair and I, now both confirmed quitters, decided to bag this job as well. Again, we hitched back to his uncle's home, giving up our short-lived worm-picking career.

It was time to shorten our stay in Montreal. I was going nuts watching Blair's uncle and wife collect and use coupons. When we walked into the dining room, we couldn't see the table.

Piles of coupons, in all sizes and colours, cut out of various magazines and papers, lay strewn across it. The kitchen counters were also covered with masses of coupons. They were everywhere in the house. One day, when Blair and I went shopping for food with his aunt and uncle, their car was jammed with maybe five hundred coupons giving discounts on everything from huge bottles of Coke to deodorant. Rather than get what they wanted, they took coupons in hand and went looking for the related products to save a few cents. They were the thriftiest couple I had ever seen.

When Blair suggested telling his uncle that we would be out of there the next morning, I readily agreed. We both thanked them sincerely for letting us stay in their home with little notice. They were perhaps a bit eccentric but very kind toward us. We decided to dump my mother's old suitcase with Blair's uncle, and his family was happy for the gift. Since we still had a lot of hitching to do, we stuffed the remaining canned goods into each of our packs. Who knew when a canned ham might come in handy?

Our hitchhiking sign continued to perform wonders. Walking just a block from Blair's uncle's home, we once again put out the sign, even though we were temporarily heading west for Ontario. Like clockwork, someone stopped within ten minutes. The moment Blair and I jumped in the car, the driver began with "Well, kids, are you really going to Europe? Do you know you are heading in the wrong direction? I was in Europe once. Let me tell you all about it. I would really recommend it. Are you sure you are going to Europe?"

Repeatedly, our drivers would drone on like this, but heck, at least we got a ride.

There were just ten more days until our student ship left port in New York, and we wished it was tomorrow. Luckily,

Blair had found a long-lost cousin who lived in New Jersey, and he had arranged for us to stay there for four nights prior to departure. With six days to fill, we hitched to the home of a cousin of mine in southern Ontario, then to Washington, DC, to see the sights. From DC we made it to Atlantic City, where we happened to stumble into a bar where The Drifters were playing their megahit, "Down by the Boardwalk." We managed to hear a few songs before we were promptly thrown out for not buying a required second beer.

6

Das Boot

I was hitchhiking the other day
And a hearse stopped.
I said, "No thanks,
I'm not going that far."

— Steven Wright

A rriving in New Jersey, we immediately left our hosts and hitched into Manhattan, spending the day looking up into a skyscraper world that didn't exist in Kelowna. We were just marking time. In four days, we would board our student ship in New York and head for England. We couldn't sleep from the excitement.

The next day, we managed to get tickets to a Yankees game in, of course, Yankee Stadium. Our seats were a few rows from the very top and gave us a fantastic view of the entire stadium, which I swore must have seated sixty thousand people. It did take a while to see the actual players on the field, who were miles from our seats, but just being there in that atmosphere of avid sports fans was thrilling.

Two nights before our ship was to leave New York, we found the name of it, the good ship *Aurelia*, in a New York newspaper that listed all the vessels docked in the city that day. We could not resist seeing it, so early the next morning, we hitched into Manhattan again and walked to the pier where our ship was docked. And there it was. I can still remember the exhilaration of staring at the *Aurelia*, our means of escaping North America for as long as we wanted. It represented unbridled freedom. Although the ship lacked paint and had signs of rust everywhere, to us it was a magnificent sight.

The good ship *Aurelia* at the pier in New York the day before we jumped aboard.

The *Aurelia* could carry up to a thousand students. And we would be two of those thousand to be whisked away to Europe! Later, we would learn that our ship was not fast at all — a snail's pace might describe its speed. The *Queen Mary*, on its way to England, could have easily lapped us. Nevertheless, the *Aurelia* did have one fabulous feature: it was cheap.

Late that afternoon, while hitching back from Manhattan, Blair and I used our sign, "Help Us To Europe," for the last time. It was no longer pure white; it looked a tad grey from dirt.

The red paint had started to fade. Still, it had become part of us whenever we were on the road and had served us well. By this point, we had received more than sixty rides while hitchhiking, and almost all the drivers had asked about the sign. Though we had tired of explaining that we were indeed going to Europe and listing the countries we planned on visiting, we had become used to the routine. That evening, after reaching Blair's cousin's house, we held a little commemorative ceremony for the death of our sign. Quietly, we slipped it under their porch.

Finally, our departure day had come. That morning we arrived at the pier to board the ship with our backpacks, passports and most of our money. The people getting on looked a few years older than us, and we heard a lot of German, Dutch and English accents. After a long wait in line, we wound our way to the area where we were to be processed and then taken to our rooms. I soon realized that something was different: we were asked to go down a flight of stairs to our room when everyone else ahead of us had gone upstairs to theirs. We ended up going down two flights of stairs to what one might call the basement, or hold, of the ship. Through a narrow, dark hallway, we finally found the door to the room where we would spend the next eight days.

Our room was about ten by ten feet and had two metal bunk beds. It was a room for four, not two. Between the beds was about four feet of space, with roughly two feet of space above the upper bed. The bathroom was far down the hall, shared with passengers like us on the bottom deck. There was no furniture in the room, simply because there was no space for it. No window, of course, since we were under sea level. *Cozy* would be a generous description of it.

But we didn't care. Blair and I thought the room was just fine. At first, I assumed that all rooms on cruise ships were like this, until I saw the ones of more affluent passengers. One deluxe room had real beds, not bunk beds, and pieces of furniture, as well as a large window where you could actually see the ocean. But none of the rooms were close to luxurious, because this was a student ship, and they had crammed in about nine hundred passengers. It was full.

Besides, Blair and I were not planning to spend even a second in our room other than passing out at night, so who cared about the lack of space or privacy? We were able to stuff our large packs under the beds and waited for our roommates, who showed up right after us. Both were a few years older and from California. They were also quite good-looking and seemed to attract a number of women on the ship, which was not exactly crawling with girls. Blair and I found this frustrating, especially since we were getting nowhere attracting the opposite sex. Just like us, our roommates had grabbed a room like this because it was the cheapest on the boat. Later, we found out they had more money than us for a trip to Europe lasting just two months. We came to find out that everyone on board had more money than us.

The ship was Italian and all the staff European. That first evening we had a feast. I could not believe how good the food was, with multiple courses, including pasta dishes and, believe it or not, free wine. This must have been the continental European influence. Due to our meagre budget, the free wine was a huge benefit for Blair and me. That night, we drank all we could at the table, but getting more wine served to us became an issue. Despite numerous requests for just one more bottle for our table, we were always met with the same answer: no.

We were assigned to tables of eight. There were women on board, but after a closer examination on our first night, Blair and I discovered a ratio of about two men to every woman.

Not good odds, but still, with nine hundred passengers, that was around three hundred women. Our table of eight, as luck would have it, was all male. The story of my life at that point.

After dinner, a ship's band would start playing dance music and a dance was held. About half the people on the boat attended the dance on our first night, and the odds of two men for every female held constant on the dance floor. Try as we might, both Blair and I struck out. We retreated to the upper deck, where a boisterous drinking party was underway, and bought one beer. *One* was the operative word, since the cost of even one beer was a luxury for us. We tried to make the single beer last the whole night, while watching well-off European students buy drink after drink well into the night.

On deck shortly after departure, Blair and our new friend, Martin from Amsterdam, who briefed us on the Heineken Brewery tours.

The next day was spent on the top deck, making friends and learning a lot about the world. There was a large contingent of Dutch students on board, and they all insisted that we visit the number-one attraction in Amsterdam, the Heineken Brewery tour. After talking all day, we headed to the dining room, where we had another great meal with our tablemates. Our snarky waiter, once again, told us our table had been served enough wine for the night and refused to bring us more of the free stuff.

As dinner ended, it was hard not to notice that a half-bottle of red wine sat on the now empty table right next to us. It stood out like a sore thumb. I looked around at other tables where people were departing, and they seemed to be leaving partially full bottles of red wine too. A light bulb went on above my head. I leaned to Blair and said, "Why don't we just help ourselves to the wine left on the other empty tables around us before the waiters take it away? It's just sitting there, waiting to be thrown out by the waiters. We can grab the wine now and drink it later."

Blair whispered back just two words: "I'm in."

I had my eye on two tables with excess wine. Blair and I both snuck over to those tables, quickly grabbed the half-full bottles and brought them back to stash under our chairs. Now we each had a new half-bottle of wine. But that really wasn't enough, since my idea was to take the wine up to the party deck after we struck out at the dance. I noticed that now the dinner was finished, few of the waiters were hanging around, having cleared most of the tables. Taking advantage of the now almost empty room, we got up to leave, picked up our own wine glasses and our half-full bottles of wine and attacked a few tables on the way out. We grabbed those half-empty wine glasses and poured the wine into our bottles. Before you could say, "More wine, please," we had two full bottles of wine. It might not have been all the same kind of red wine, but it was all red and very suitable for our purposes. We managed to get our newfound stash down to our room without being detected and headed for the dance.

As expected, Blair and I both struck out with the women again. But smiling this time, we went back down to our room and brought our two 'borrowed' bottles of wine and wine glasses up to the party deck. We were even generous, allowing others to partake in our sort-of-blended wine (we may have combined a Pinot Noir with a Bordeaux for an exciting new taste). Unlike the prior night, when we had nursed a beer, we were able to drink all night and enjoy the evening.

Over the next few nights, we got the wine game down to perfection. We progressed to filling up three bottles of wine a night, forcing a used cork into the bottle of wine with our hands. Once on the party deck, to make it appear as if we had just purchased the wine, we used a borrowed corkscrew to open each bottle with a lot of noise and fanfare. We became a little less picky in getting our wine, switching from trying to find bottles with wine in them to just circling a good table (meaning a table that didn't drink much wine) after everyone had left, and emptying every glass of red into our own bottle.

Like a good sports competition, this was a timed event. Blair and I didn't want to be discovered by those who supervised the dinner and have them end our wine source prematurely. We tried to do the entire operation in less than a minute and were always nearly the last to leave the dining room. After the first two nights, we brought up four used glasses to the party, rather than two, hoping to find a few thirsty damsels and entertain them on our blended wine concoction.

After day three, we were well-liked and fell into a routine. It went something like this: Get up late, when the bathrooms were free, just in time for lunch. Spend the afternoon on deck learning about where to go in Europe, then arrive right on time for dinner. Try the dance and strike out, party up on deck with our ample supply of wine, handle rejection from the women we had plied with our wine and pass out around three in the morning in our closet-like room. Repeat the next night.

At the dance on our last night, I met Karen, a young woman from London, England. She had been to a US university on an exchange after her first year of post-secondary schooling in Britain. I invited her for a tad bit of wine up on deck with Blair and me, and she accepted. As the night wore on, we talked and talked, and perhaps drank a bit too much. Blair got hammered and told me he was heading for bed, which was very unusual, as he was usually one of the last to leave.

Finally, around 3:00 a.m., I convinced Karen that she might like to see our wonderful cabin, and she agreed. I couldn't believe my luck. Unfortunately, when I opened the door to our room, I could smell the distinct odour of vomit. Blair was the only one in the room, snoring away, spread out over a lower bunk that was not even his. In the space between the two bunks were pretty much all of his stomach contents on the floor.

You couldn't last a second in that room.

On to plan B — but there really was no plan B. Karen and I simply talked the rest of the night away back up on deck. She told me she had been brought up with a rather privileged lifestyle just outside of London. She found America to be rather basic compared to the sophistication of London. I compared her upbringing to mine in small-town Kelowna. Quite a contrast.

Standing on the deck together, we watched our good ship *Aurelia* pull into the harbour in Southampton at 6:30 a.m., eight days after we had left New York. At last we were here. After all the dreaming and planning, I was now only a few hours from walking down a gangplank to England. It was the real start of our trip. I could see only old warehouses and a lot of cement from my vantage point on the deck of the ship, but was sure the England of green rolling hills and magnificent old buildings I had dreamed about was just beyond the horizon.

Karen went on and on about how quaint rural England was in contrast to the sophistication of London. She was somewhat condescending in describing the small towns, rolling hills and its rural citizens, but I loved it. I could have jumped off the boat right then to start our trip. But then I would have been leaving Blair behind, who was still passed out in our cabin. That morning, Karen was taking the train to London, where her parents lived just outside of the city. Just before she left, she invited us to stay in their house for a night when we got to London. Though foiled by Blair's unfortunate illness in our room, at least we had yet another free night in England.

To Europe

Arriving in Southampton, England, in the summer of '64, our hitchhiking route ended in Gothenburg, where we bought an old Saab. You can see the ill-fated Saab's route to Luxembourg, where we dumped the Saab and once again moved forward by thumb. Our hitchin' route took us all the way down to the southwest edge of Europe, to the Territory of Gibraltar.

Mode of Travel

Hitchhiking
Travellers' own car
Boat

7

Long-Lost Relatives

I haven't been everywhere, but it's on my list.

— Susan Sontag

As soon as Blair woke up, we were off to hitch to a distant cousin's cottage just outside of Southampton and hopefully stay the night. I had no idea who she was, nor her exact relation to me, but I had written in advance to tell her we would show up on the day our ship arrived in Southampton. We were the last passengers off the ship, since Blair was a bit under the weather. In fact, he was more than just under the weather. He was a disaster. I suggested he take another hour in the shower, but he told me he had already been in the shower for a good hour and it was doing nothing for him. He could hardly walk. I was not doing any better, as I had not slept for twenty-four hours. The lack of sleep and a bit of wine were all catching up with me. Together, we stumbled off the ship with our packs and started hitchhiking a few miles in the direction, we hoped, of my cousin's cottage. However, just standing up, a hitchhiking prerequisite, was difficult.

After hitching in circles for a long time, we finally found the cottage, only ten miles from the harbour as the crow flies (but then, we were not crows).

Knocking on what I hoped was the right door, we were met with two faces that might be described as who-the-hell-are-you? types. When she opened the door, my relative asked cautiously, "Yes?"

"Oh, I hope you got our letters," I replied quickly. "I am Jim Kerr and this is my friend Blair, and my mother's maiden name is Mary Little. I hope you were expecting us?"

Not a move from either of them. They just stood at the door. I babbled on. "My mother often talks about you." (This was complete bull, of course.) "I hope we are not intruding." (I already knew we were.)

Finally, after staring me up and down for what seemed forever, surveying my wrinkled shirt and dirty jeans, my relative said, "Well, I guess you'd better come in, then."

I jumped at the delayed invitation. "Thank you so much. My mother will want to know all about you. It's so nice we can stay with you." (I thought I should lay the groundwork that we wanted to stay the night.)

Under the circumstances, all went reasonably well, until I apparently started snoring in their living room within ten minutes of arrival, meaning Blair had to carry on the conversation by himself. When the snoring got louder and louder, Blair tried to wake me up, but apparently I was completely gone.

Blair and I were never formally invited to spend the night, as I recall. After they had graciously fed us dinner, where we asked numerous questions about England, all answered with one or two words, my relatives explained that they did not have a guest room. They offered to drive us to a nearby youth hostel instead. This was not the plan. I countered with something like

"That's okay, we don't need a guest room. We can just roll out our sleeping bags on your living room floor. We will be quite comfortable."

And that's what we did.

The next morning, we got out of there as early as we could. Looking back, I had come a long way in just one month of travel. My confidence had grown and I had begun taking initiatives I would never have taken before leaving Kelowna. If this had been the first day of our trip, I would have thanked my relatives profusely for offering to drive us to the local youth hostel and left their home, happy as a clam. But by this time, Blair and I had become somewhat more assertive. We were not yet what I would call pushy, but teetering perilously close.

We had a set amount of money, and we wanted to maximize the number of days we were travelling. As the weeks had gone by since we left Kelowna, a new Jim was breaking out of his old shell. Already the trip was having a major effect on my personality. I no longer feared confrontation, and though not looking forward to it, I could handle it far better than before.

As we quickly walked to the outskirts of Southampton to hitchhike north, Blair and I reflected on our many conversations about money with our fellow shipmates. Almost to a man, everyone thought we were crazy to try and travel on just two dollars a day. Most were budgeting ten dollars a day or more, and they found two dollars a day laughable. An alternative for us was to cut the length of our trip in half and spend twice as much money a day. But we quickly dismissed that option, as it meant cutting out so many places we wanted to see, and the journey had just begun.

Besides, the next ten nights were all free, with another relative and our London pen pals. We would just need to explain to our pen pals we had zero money and cut costs where we could.

If need be, we might get a job later on. We were going to stick it out no matter·what and were determined not to come home early. We were going to give our meagre budget a try. Even if it meant sleeping on the side of the road.

Our next lucky relative lived in Bath, which happened to be on the way to London, our next destination. I had written them earlier saying that Blair and I would be arriving the day after docking in Southampton. With little difficulty, we found my cousin in Bath, with their true English cottage with walls a yard thick and a thatched roof.

A giant of a man with a big smile opened the door when I knocked. "You must be Jim. We've been expecting you. You boys must be starved. Would you like a beer?" What a contrast to the greeting we had received yesterday.

Unlike my distant cousin in Southampton, these folks actually seemed pleased to see us, gave us a warm beer and immediately showed us to our bedroom. It was late in the day and they went on and on, saying that we could not leave Bath without spending a day seeing their famous cathedral and other great sights of Bath and enjoying their cooking skills. It was now two nights in Bath, delaying our arrival time in London by a day. We hated to leave such welcoming hosts disappointed.

The Bath cathedral was indeed amazing. It had been constructed over many hundreds of years, burned down and rebuilt again. Reportedly it was one of the finest examples of Gothic churches in the world. Of course, never having seen a church this big in my life, I couldn't give two hoots if it was Gothic or some other type of architecture. I didn't even know what Gothic was. It was the first of many religious buildings that I saw on our trip, but because it was the first, I can still picture it today. I wondered how much it must have cost the poor citizens to construct this monument as a symbol to God and to display His greatness. It seemed like the cathedral's construction was more about humbling the locals than celebrating God's magnificence. The buildings were indeed magnificent, but at what cost? How many lives were lost just building these monuments? How many peasants gave up their wages to pay for this? What if all these sums had instead been given back to them? Would their lives have been better or worse?

As a child, I had been slightly religious. Once, while attending the United Church Sunday-school class in Kelowna, I was accused of stealing money from the donation bowl. I had cupped my hand over the bowl to hide my donation of twenty-five cents, just like I had seen my father do when he attended church twice a year. I was asked to empty my pockets. They expected to find half the contents of the donation bowl stuffed into my shorts. Finding nothing, they started yelling at me, wondering how a clever lad like me had managed to hide his loot prior to being caught. Where was it? It took a half hour for them to believe me, even after I had explained my father's trick of hiding his donation. From that day onwards, I wasn't too sure about God and the people who worked in that church. They certainly were not into forgiveness and seemed more interested in money and control.

As I got older, I grew more skeptical. By the time I was at university, I was agnostic. A few years later, I stood firmly in the atheist camp. It wasn't that I didn't think the Church did a world of good. It stood for goodness and right, and that was fine. Yet Christianity's origin myths and miraculous tales seemed like a gigantic, well, myth to me.

8

London

In life, it's not where you go — it's who you travel with.

— Charles M. Schultz

A day later than expected, we arrived at the doorstep of our first pen pal in London. Jane welcomed us with open arms and a barrage of questions about our trip so far. She was twenty years old, just a year older than me, and attending a local college. She still lived with her parents, who were just as nice as her. In the first half hour, I think she never stopped smiling. Their flat was about thirty-five minutes by train from the centre of London. Best of all, it had a spare room just large enough to fit two sleeping bags.

That evening, her family told us they wanted to take us out for a traditional English dinner. Rather than get in their car, we simply walked two blocks to their neighbourhood pub. This was our first-ever visit to a pub. This one looked at least a hundred years old, with low ceilings, dark black beams and small, inviting corner nooks everywhere. There must have been fifty people packed into the place, all talking at once. After greeting at least five others, Jane's father found a table and asked Blair and me what we wanted. We replied, "A beer," of course. But this was not the right answer. He wanted to know if we wanted an ale, a bitter, a stout, or perhaps an IPA. Realizing we hadn't a clue, he told us that he would get us a pint of traditional British beer.

He came back from the bar, beers in hand. "I've got you lads a couple of pints of dark brown ale, brewed just a few miles from here. It'll put hair on your chest. It's got to be the favourite in the pub. Cheers."

The beer was a complete surprise — it was lukewarm. Secondly, it was dark brown. Really brown. Not willing to offend our gracious host, who was paying, I said nothing and sipped it down, saying yes to another later in the evening. It wasn't until a few days later that I realized they always served their beer lukewarm in England, so you could taste it, unlike in Canada, where it was served cold and somewhat tasteless. As friends came by our table, Jane's father introduced us as young lads from the colonies visiting his daughter. Everyone was overly friendly. We all had beef pie and even more beer as the night wore on. The pie was a lot better than the beer. During a break, I whispered to Blair that we had done very well picking Jane as our first pen pal. At the end of the evening, I decided that I would be a happy camper to spend all my days in a British pub for the rest of our trip. Alcohol consumption was a theme recurring from the previous leg of our journey at sea and perhaps the start of a bit of extra imbibing for the rest of my life.

The next day, Jane took the day off to show us the many sights of London, including Piccadilly Circus, Tower Bridge, Westminster Cathedral and St. Paul's. Later, we walked the streets of London and boarded the evening boat for a cruise on the River Thames. This pen pal thing was a very good idea.

Blair with our packs taking in the scene at Piccadilly Circus in London. Notice the movie advertisement for the silver-screen hit *The Unsinkable Molly Brown*.

We stayed two nights and most of the third day, then moved on to pen pal number two, Elizabeth. With four pen pals to visit in eight days, that left two nights per pen pal. All were women. We had given each a range of dates in advance. Blair and I had worked out the order in which we would visit each one, starting with what we thought was the best situation. We would see how our first pen pal worked out before saying we would spend just one day or two days with her, then move on.

Elizabeth lived in the other end of London, about an hour by the Tube. She lived with her family in a row house, right across from a small park. Like Jane, Elizabeth was a happy camper, bubbling over, saying how pleased she was that we were able to stay with her at her parents' home for a couple of days. She, too, had planned a full day of sightseeing and talked a mile a minute about all the sights we would jam into a day, including Piccadilly Circus and the Tower Bridge.

Blair and I made the mistake of not telling Elizabeth that we had already been in London for three days. As a result, we were trapped the next day when she took us to see Piccadilly Circus (again), Westminster Abbey (again), Tower Bridge (again) and luckily also Hyde Park and Buckingham Palace, to see the changing of the guard. We had a great time, but time was of the essence. The next day, we moved on to pen pal number three.

Despite how fascinating Piccadilly Circus was, I could not stand being taken there a third time, so we told our new, lovely, charming pen pal, Judith, that we had been in London for five days, staying with a relative, but were so looking forward to meeting her and her family.

Judith's family lived close to the city in a large brick duplex. She was the youngest of four, and all her brothers and sisters had flown the coop. She must have been six feet tall and wore the largest pair of glasses I have ever seen. She and her mother and father could not have been happier to see us. Once again, we got the barrage of questions of where we had been and how we liked London. Once again, a jackpot.

The next day, Judith took us to some of the more educational sights, like the National Museum, the Tate Gallery and some more art galleries, to more pubs, and for a long walk along the Thames. Judith told us she was in a third-year arts program at a small private university in London. Hanging around her and visiting all of these museums and art galleries was starting to rub off. In short, Blair and I felt we were becoming quite sophisticated.

Our time with our fourth pen pal, Wendy, was different. Again, we told her and her parents that we had already been in the city and done most of the tourist sights. Her father was a producer at the British Broadcasting Corporation (BBC). He suggested that rather than see the sights again, we might like to spend the next day at the BBC studio watching a new TV series being filmed. Bingo! We leapt at the chance. The day at the film studio was a highlight for us. After spending the entire day with Wendy's father, we went out with a few of her pals, including her new boyfriend, to the neighbourhood pub. Wendy was vivacious, attractive and the centre of our group. We were no experts on British pubs and found that this one was just like the others: friendly and full of patrons. Blair and I were so happy that toward the end of the night, we even bought a round for Wendy and her friends. We had spent money on little else.

So, it was London for eight days on less than three pounds (about the equivalent of six Canadian dollars, far below even our skimpy budget). Yes, we were a bit cheap, to say the least, but at least I wrote each pen pal after our stay to thank them and explain that because Blair and I had so little money, we couldn't afford to take them out and hoped they understood.

But, and this was a big *but*, I added we would both soon return in a subsequent year and take them out for an extravagant meal on us. Of course, things changed and we never did get back to buy those meals, but at least I offered.

London opened our eyes to what a big city was like. Quite a contrast to Kelowna, a town of ten thousand people. I loved looking at the sights of the city for the first time in my life. However, I did have a little problem with heights, which should have tipped me off not to climb up higher than ten feet on any church or monument.

St. Paul's was where the problem first arose. A magnificent cathedral, it has a dome like nothing I had ever seen before. You can walk up an inside staircase to the dome, which I did without any thought, and come out to a catwalk surrounding it, about ninety feet above the floor of the church. When I walked out of the little entrance door, then five or six feet more to the edge of a railing that circled the dome, I just about died. The railing only came up to my waist, not nearly high enough, in my opinion. My immediate urge was to jump off the catwalk to the floor. Bolts of fear were shooting through my body. I was in a full sweat and froze. After a few minutes, I was able to gather myself and step backwards, very slowly, toward the entrance to the stairs I had just come up, so that I could run down those stairs to the bottom floor.

I made it to the top of the stairs, feeling very relieved, and turned around to start the descent. However, the guard at the door told me that the only way down was on the other side of the dome. These stairs were for going up only. He was not to be persuaded by someone panicky, feeling close to death, with sweat all over his face and body. His only job was to prevent those wanting to go down from using these stairs. He was not going to sacrifice his job for a nineteen-year-old with sweaty features.

I froze, of course, and tried to figure out how I was going to get halfway across this catwalk to the other side of the dome, where the downward stairs were located. I could see over the railing, and it was a long drop to the floor. Finally, I got up the nerve to move about a foot sideways, then another foot, with my legs, bum, back and head all firmly pressed as hard as I could against the back wall of the dome. Gradually, after twenty minutes of pure sweat, I moved the few hundred feet needed to get to the downwards entrance on the other side. My backside never left the comfort of being jammed against the wall of the dome. At last, I ran down the correct stairs, only to be met by Blair's mocking laughter. He had come down much earlier and was wondering how I had got stuck up there. I was so relieved to be on solid ground, his response had no effect on me.

Over those eight days and nights in London, we were in British pubs for dinner three times, cruised the river twice, saw Piccadilly Square twice, etc. You get the idea. It was wonderful, and all four pen pals were great. But it was time to move on. First, however, we needed to take up the offer from Karen, the girl from the ship, to stay a night at her home, which was situated in a suburb of London. How difficult could it be to find a house only forty miles outside the city?

In two words: very difficult. Blair and I headed out by Tube to where Karen lived. We couldn't find the street on our map but knew the general area where the home should be located. We ended up in a neighbourhood of rolling hills, with very large estate-type homes on lots of well over an acre, protected by eight-foot-high rock walls and large metal gates. In many cases, it was difficult just to find the address of the home when standing right in front of the gate. Our strategy changed to simply asking everyone we saw if they had ever heard of the street. After what seemed forever, I found someone who knew the street. We walked for miles and eventually found the house, together with its gate and high walls. We rang the bell.

Karen was excited to see us both, and we were only a day late. But her mother was not pleased and gave us a rather icy reception. We did have a rather formal dinner and a good chat about British politics.

The next day, Karen explained that her mother was not too keen on anyone her daughter met. Having a potential boyfriend actually stay in the house was going over the top. She told me that because she had invited us to the house for a night, her mother had jumped to the conclusion that there might be a romance going on here. There was not, and I was far from the material that her mother thought suitable for her daughter, hence her reception. We did see how the other half lived, though. A different experience than with our pen pals, and too formal an atmosphere for Blair and me. After what they would call a "lovely lunch" in the garden, served by their maid, we gathered our grubby old packs and hit the road. It was time to head north.

9

On the Road Again

For my part, I travel not to go anywhere, but to go. I travel for travel's sake. The great affair is to move.

— Robert Louis Stevenson

Our first day of hitching out of London started off poorly. We were not sure where the hell we were going. Just as we got on the road, it started pouring and poured all day. There is nothing worse than hitchhiking in the rain. First, you look like drowned rats to someone who might consider giving you a lift. Why would they want soaking-wet rats sitting in their car? Our only hope was to find someone who felt sorry for us, who might stop just to get us out of the rain. We needed to find a spot on the highway where the cars had to slow down to see our smiling, wet faces. With no sign to help us, rides were harder to find. Our thick canvas packs were indestructible, but in a rain, they just soaked up the wetness. You could have poured an entire bucket of water on my pack and not a drop would have ended up on the ground.

Changing direction, we decided to head for the nearest town with a youth hostel, about fifteen miles away and roughly eighty miles north of London.

Splurging, we checked into the first room on our trip where we had to pay. It had been forty nights so far, and every one of them had been free. At this point, Blair and I had spent next to nothing and were way ahead of our budget. But still frugal, we got a room that slept four, cheaper than a room for two. We spread all of our wet stuff, including my walking shoes, which were soaked right through, everywhere around the room.

Soon we were joined by our roommates, who were from southern England. For most of the night, we chatted about the differences between universities in England and Canada — a scintillating topic. I had barely scraped through first-year English, taught by a PhD candidate, not a full professor. My new roommate thought that using PhD students to teach first-year classes just showed how short-staffed my university was. My 'fake' prof, in fact, was excellent, and I would never have gotten through the course without him.

When we finally went to bed, there was a bad odour in the room, like a dead fish left out in the sun to rot. With everyone in bed, one of the guys who had joined us asked, "What the hell is that bad smell? It's unbelievable. I can't sleep with that smell in the air. Where the hell is that odour coming from?"

I cringed and rolled over, fearing that the smell must be coming from my wet, worn-out shoes.

"Found it," he said loudly. "Whose shoes are sitting on the windowsill? They stink to high heaven. Get these shoes out of here."

I decided it might be best to fess up that they were mine. I took them outside to an area covered by a large veranda, in case the rain started up again. I snuck back into the room, rolled over and pretended that nothing had happened, but could hear muffled laughter from Blair, which bugged the hell out of me. My feet did sweat a lot. Combined with soaking from the rain, this made for a very unpleasant smell.

The next morning, the smelly shoes incident seemed to dominate our breakfast conversation. Blair gave me no help at all in fending off the complaints. As I remember it, all he did was laugh.

My shoes were crucial to my trip. I tried cleaning them, since they were my only ones, other than a pair of moccasins that I wore indoors. Despite the persistent smell, I kept those shoes for another month before they fell apart. Later, the quest for new shoes would even cause Blair and me to split up for a few days.

Mailing a letter to my mother, I asked her if she could buy me a new pair of shoes and send them to me poste restante to Berlin, where we were certain to visit our pen pal from that city. (*Poste restante*, French for "waiting mail," means the post office will hold your mail for a specified period of time.) Poste restante was how we received all our mail from home. The advantage of it was that they would forward your mail, at no cost, to the post office in the next city where you were travelling. We would guess where we would be on a certain day and ask our parents to send a letter to, say, Amsterdam poste restante. About half the time, their letter would be waiting. If it was not there, we would provide instructions to the post office to forward our missing letter to the next city we thought we would find ourselves in, and so on. This was how I planned on handling receiving my new shoes.

Blair and I decided to try to hitch all the way to Edinburgh without stopping. By this time, we had been hitching so much that it was becoming a bit too routine. As a lark, and to liven things up a little on the way to Edinburgh, we decided to switch names. Blair would be Jim and I would be Blair. We tried it out on our first ride. Blair introduced himself as Jim and I as Blair to our unsuspecting driver. It was a lot harder than you think, because as soon as our driver said "Jim," I would react before Blair. It is hard to remain silent when your name is called.

Our thought was to keep this going after more practice on the road, so that when we met our pen pal, we would have it down pat. It would get a bit tricky, as Blair pretending to be Jim would need to know exactly what I had told the pen pal about myself (which, of course, I'd forgotten) and react every time he said "Jim." It's far harder than it sounds, and we managed to truly piss off a driver on one of our rides when he discovered we were playing a game on him. As I recall, showing no regard for the skill our exchange required, he stopped the car and threw us out — with our packs, thank God.

Despite our Scottish ancestry and presumed affinity for the land, Scotland was a bit of a bust. Perhaps it was the constant rain, or maybe we were just tired of the sights of Great Britain and wanted to get on to the continent. We did have a brief stop in Edinburgh to visit our last pen pal in Great Britain, and managed to pull off our name change. The city of Edinburgh was both beautiful and charming, but we were getting itchy for Europe. Sadly, this was our only urban stop in Scotland, because somehow I had lost the address of our pen pal in Glasgow. Without telling Blair, I had turned my pack upside down looking for the address, and for some reason it was not with the addresses of all the other pen pals. This might have been the first indication that my organizational abilities were a tad wanting.

After two days, we were off, thumbing our way to Dover to catch a ferry to the continent. Our first ride out of Edinburgh, heading south, was in a large Jaguar sedan. The driver was a dentist. He told us that yes, Edinburgh was lovely, but if you wanted to make money in Scotland, you worked in Glasgow. After you had enough, you retired in Edinburgh. The fellow was obviously well off. Blair told me right after the ride that he might consider dentistry when he went to university. His mother had always wanted him to be a dentist. He had dismissed the career until now, but I could tell he was giving dentistry a second look after listening to this chap and seeing his car. I used the occasion to remind him that my father wanted me to be an engineer. Look where that had taken me. (In the end, Blair got a degree in commerce and ended up in marketing.)

Once you start on the cheap circuit, as I would call our trip, you gravitate to a lot of others who are doing the same thing. I never did find anyone who was spending less money a day to survive than we were, but I discovered that the people you meet in the cheapest place in town can really help you on your next destination. For example, we were going to Amsterdam next, and someone who had just been there told us where in the city was the best place to stay. Often, the youth hostel was not the cheapest or best place to stay, and no one we had met previously on our trip would be there. They would all be in a less expensive but nicer hotel, perhaps down the street.

Word of mouth, or the jungle telegraph, as we called it, was good for everything. Everyone would know the cheapest rooming house or hotel in each city. If we needed to find the cheapest fare to get across the channel, someone just around the corner would know the exact ferry, when it left and what it cost. If it meant leaving at 3:00 a.m. and sitting in a lifeboat, that's what we would do. The funny thing is that when you do end up going on a dilapidated 3:00 a.m. ferry, you tend to know a lot of people in the lineup, since they, too, have been told this was the best deal around.

That night we hitched as quickly as possible down to Dover and crossed the Channel on some beat-up boat to Calais, France. The ferry took less than three hours to cross.

The first road sign we saw in Calais showed distances to nearby cities, but it looked way out of whack. Right away, I realized why: distances were now in kilometres, not miles.

Having grown up using miles my entire life, I was not familiar at all with how long a kilometre was. That day, we soon figured out that a kilometre was about half the length of a mile. Therefore, we just divided everything by two to give us a rough estimate of how far we had to hitch. Later, we adjusted this trick to a closer approximation of miles by multiplying the number of kilometres by .6 to get the equivalent in miles. We were never able to think in kilometres. After we saw the number of kilometres posted, it was always "How many damn miles away is our destination?"

The next day, we hitched right up to Amsterdam and splurged and stayed in their youth hostel, one of the largest and liveliest we experienced during our whole trip.

10

Free Beer

Drink heavily with locals whenever possible.

— *Anthony Bourdain*

In those days, among our crowd, Amsterdam was famous for two things: the Heineken Brewery morning tour, which was free, and the red-light district, which was not. So, Blair and I just window-shopped in the red-light district and concentrated on the brewery tour. Our plan was to be first in line at the brewery and to keep going every day until they threw us out. Word on the street was that the average time before you were thrown out was two days. Only a select few could make it to day three.

At nine sharp, we showed up for the first tour, which lasted about an hour. We were ushered into a tasting room, where in front of us were plates of various cheeses, cigarettes and all the beer you could drink. The advantage of the first tour was they didn't care what tour you were on, but they did close the tasting room sharply at noon. So, we had roughly two hours to smoke cigarettes, have a free breakfast of cheese and maybe six glasses of draft beer, and talk to our friends. If you were on the ten tour, your time in the tasting room was cut down to only one hour — a disaster. We both made sure to stuff our pockets with handfuls of cheese and a few extra cigarettes as we left, or as I should say, were pushed out the door. We were set for the day.

The people who ran the tour knew well the scam we were trying to pull off, of course, and were quite diligent in weeding out people like us who had already been on their tour and were unlikely to buy a Heineken beer in the immediate future. We were told by our gang to change our clothes and maybe wear a hat for the next day's early morning tour to avoid being turned down at the door.

Changing our clothes was not easy, as we had few, but it worked, and we did the same routine again. On the third day, we didn't want to push our luck so decided to wait a while and not take the nine tour, where some of our buddies were. Instead, we took the ten tour, under some sort of disguise, hoping they were not as diligent in policing this tour for deadbeats like us. Again, we were successful. However, in the tasting room, the gig was up. The staff recognized us as the ones who had six beers two days in a row, ate all the cheese and stole their cigarettes. We managed to suck back a quick one, put some cheese in our pockets and escape in short order. In English, they told us it would not be a good idea to come back the next day. Overall, our plan was a good scam. Without advice from others in the same circumstances, we would probably have done just one tour, starting at ten, and never have pulled off the Heineken beer caper.

Culturally, Amsterdam was far removed from any city in Canada, especially when you walked around the city after six Heinekens. Previously, I had been unaware of all the canals and museums and the large red-light district. Somehow, it all seemed far more grown-up than Canada. On our third day, Blair and I decided to see if we could get into the Rijksmuseum after our aborted beer tour. The word at the hostel was that the large painting by Rembrandt called *The Night Watch* was worth the price of admission alone. But to us, nothing was worth the price of admission, which was something like the equivalent of two dollars each, our budget for an entire day. Our goal was to get in for free somehow.

On approaching the museum's ticket window, Blair and I hoped there would be a sign saying students could enter for free. There was not. But a sign did read that for all those eighteen years or younger, there was no charge. This was great for Blair, who was eighteen, but I was the ripe age of nineteen. We needed a strategy to get in. Blair went first, showing his passport, which clearly indicated he was eighteen and qualified for a free ticket. I quickly followed. Rather than give the fellow my passport, I gave him my driver's licence, where the age was far harder to decipher. Blair was right beside me, and I tried to look as young as possible, giving him the wild grin of a twelve-year-old. The man behind the counter just waved the two of us in, giving me a prized ticket for nothing.

We headed straight for the Rembrandt painting, which, indeed, was huge. It must have been more than twelve feet wide and eight feet high. It really was worth the price of admission (nothing, in our case). After ten minutes of pretending to know what we were looking at, we were off.

This was just my fifth visit to an art gallery or museum on our trip. I quickly found that I had no patience to examine and contemplate each painting. In short, I had the attention span of a tsetse fly. It would remain the same for all future visits to museums.

It seemed that most people in Amsterdam were either riding an old-fashioned bike with the handles up in the air or walking. Vast areas were without cars, making walks along the canals fabulous. After our quick museum tour, Blair and I headed out for another walk along the canals. I couldn't stop noticing the outdoor restaurants built right alongside them. One image will remain with me forever: in a very classy restaurant with silver settings and undoubtedly expensive wine glasses, waiters wore formal suits, serving the beautiful people amazing meals on tables covered in white linen. Blair and I were so far from sitting down in such a place. We just stared and moved on.

After three days, it was time to move on again. Hearing that Copenhagen was one of the nicest cities in the world, Blair and I hitched north. It was what we expected, but the cost to survive was out of this world. It was the most expensive city we had been to on our trip. Obviously, no matter how frugal we were, living on two bucks a day in Scandinavia was impossible. We were each now up to the extravagant rate of four dollars a day. Since we wanted to travel as long as we could, this wasn't going to cut it. If we didn't come up with a solution fast, we'd have to end our trip in a month or two.

We changed our plans and thought we might get a job for two weeks in Sweden, where every young woman was blonde and perhaps anxious to meet young Canadian guys like us. Our thought was first to see Oslo, the capital of Norway, then head back to Sweden, work for two weeks and from there take the short ferry to Germany and head south. The jungle telegraph told us that Oslo was very scenic and friendly but extraordinarily expensive as well. The cheapest way to Norway was to take a ferry directly to Sweden from Denmark, then hitch our way up north. From Oslo, we would hitch back to Gothenburg, next door, then start our journey south to Germany as fall was approaching.

The hitching was good. We easily made Oslo in a day and found the youth hostel, which was expensive but seemed worth it due to its convenient location, included breakfast and gorgeous views. The hostel was on the top of a hill, with a view of the city below. It was easy to get downtown, too, as a tram went all the way at a very reasonable rate. There was some skill in making sure it was a reasonable rate, however. We would ride the tram for maybe two stops before the conductor approached us for money, then jump off and jump on the next tram for another two or three stops, staging our way to the centre of the city without paying a krona.

Blair and I began to think Oslo might be the place to work for a while. From talking to others, it seemed there was full employment in Oslo, meaning lots of temporary jobs going around. Apparently, it was easy for foreigners to get temporary jobs that paid some of the highest wages in all of Europe. Besides, we had a large, somewhat deluxe room, which partly overlooked the entire city. The hostel could not have been more than two or three years old — it even smelled new. To top it off, for breakfast we were served a feast of multiple cheeses, very healthy-looking breads and various slices of meat.

That night, after buying some local cheese and bread and bringing it back to our room for dinner, Blair and I debated whether to get a job in Oslo or wait a few days and try Sweden. We needed more money. The wages in Oslo were apparently high, the hostel was great, so why take a chance that we would find all this in Sweden?

We made the decision to get a job in Oslo the next day.

11

Rusty Joints

Live life with no excuses, travel with no regret.

— *Oscar Wilde*

The next day, the check-in staff at our youth hostel told us to visit a government employment agency, where they posted temporary positions on a job board. The agency was only a short tram ride down the hill. We charmed a clerk there, who helped us in English go over all the jobs available. We confessed to her that our high school Norwegian was a little rusty. She recommended a good one that paid a lot per hour and was for a week or a bit more: working in a scaffolding plant not far from the youth hostel. We would not need to speak Norwegian to get the job, which was perfect, as that could have been a deal-breaker. She arranged a job interview for us the following day, and off we went.

The next morning, we found the place, a plant that made joints to keep scaffolding together. We were directed to another area of the plant, which had used parts strewn everywhere. A guy who appeared to be a foreman showed us a large bin full of maybe three hundred joints, all looking very rusty and old.

Beside that, another large bin of the same size stood empty. The job was simply to oil and grease the old, dirty scaffolding joints. All we had to do was put them on an upright steel pipe and loosen them up until they were like new, using tons of oil. Once they were perfect, we were to throw them into the empty bin. For this very skilled job we were going to be paid the equivalent of about $1.30 an hour, a very high wage at the time. We would have been lucky to make eighty cents an hour in Kelowna.

The foreman, who introduced himself as Erik, seemed like a great guy and spoke some English. There was really no interview; he just wanted someone to do this unskilled job now. After little thought, we said, "Yes, we will take the job," signed a few forms, and within an hour were watching him demonstrate how to grease an old, rusty scaffolding joint. With a huge smile, Erik finished greasing one of the joints in about five minutes and tossed it into the empty bin with a flourish.

When it was our turn, we discovered that it was not as easy as it looked. For one thing, the operative word was *rusted*. These joints were *really* rusted. After picking up one joint and pouring oil all over the damn thing, I could not get it to move an inch, despite my best efforts with a huge wrench. Just holding the wrench was like lifting weights in a gym. We brought back our instructor, Erik, who showed us that we were not oiling the right spot. Soon, with a smile, he started moving all the parts, and in about five minutes, he threw the second scaffolding joint into the empty bin.

Blair and I were to work side by side, sitting on stools, with a vertical pipe in front of us where we would mount the scaffolding joint. With hundreds of rusty joints in a bin on our left and an almost empty bin on our right, we both tackled the job with gusto. In about ten minutes, or maybe more, we each managed to make one joint operational. We threw our now working scaffolding joints into the empty bin at the same time, like a basketball heading for the hoop. Our new friend Erik came over for a look and gave us a big smile and thumbs-up. From that point on, we got faster and faster.

Luckily it was a union shop, and coffee breaks must have lasted twenty minutes, with a long lunch break as well. At the end of the day, Blair and I were experts at rusty scaffolding restoration. In the last hour, we started to have a contest to see who could oil a joint the fastest. However, as we were leaving for the day, we realized that if we kept this pace up, our eight-day job would be over in four days. Once all those rusty scaffolding joints had been oiled and made whole again, our job was over. Since we were getting paid by the hour, it became obvious that the longer we took, the more we would get paid.

The next day, we got a huge break. Erik asked if we could teach him a bit of English. We agreed. We naturally couldn't work while the lesson was on, so we kept these lessons going as long as we could and started teaching him jokes in English, which he loved and practised on us. Every time he screwed up a joke, Blair and I laughed and laughed, despite not having a clue what he had said. We would ask him about his family and found that the more questions we asked, the more he would smile and show pictures of his children, wife, dog and great-aunt.

In teaching Erik English, Blair and I found that constant praise worked wonders. He was really trying, since it was important to him to learn some English. The day after 'a lesson', he would always tell us that he used a few new English words on his wife. When she didn't understand, he took great pleasure in explaining to her, in Norwegian, what the new words meant and demonstrating how he was now getting educated.

The other strategy that really worked, and took up a lot of time, was taking an interest in how Erik could roll a cigarette with one hand in less than thirty seconds, using his own cigarette paper and a pouch of tobacco. The finished cigarette looked perfect. Blair and I would try for hours with both hands, and they were nowhere close to perfect. But while we were practising rolling cigarettes and teaching him English, not a single rusty scaffolding joint moved from the dirty to the clean bin. Blair and I stopped racing each other as well. We gave out mock awards to each other on who could do the slowest job and still look very busy. We managed to stretch out the job for eight full days. The downside was that after seven days, the charm of this job had worn off. Though we never mastered the art of rolling a cigarette with one hand, we got pretty good at it with both hands.

The highlight, though, was Erik. He had such a great sense of humour and was genuinely interested in us and our travels. Erik's English improved a lot in those eight days. Blair and I congratulated him and gave him a fake certificate of graduation from our 'college'.

To avoid having a lot of taxes withheld from our paycheque, Blair and I had to get a special form from the government as part-time foreign workers. With big smiles, we each cashed a cheque for a net payment of 278 kroner, about the equivalent of $65. It might not sound like much, but considering we started with around $380 for our trip, it was a big improvement to our financial situation. We felt like kings. Once again, we converted the money into American Express travellers' cheques of $10 each. In Oslo, and everywhere we went, we would each cash the rough equivalent of $10 into Norwegian krona at a local bank, hide that money in our secret money pouches until it was gone, then repeat.

Oslo was a wonderful city. At maybe two kilometres square, it was small enough that after a few days we had learned our way around. Everyone seemed happy, without any panhandlers or a scrap of garbage on the streets. With our newfound wealth, we went out to a few bars at night, some dances and night clubs, and even went for dinner at a restaurant.

Blair and I both thought back to an idea we had had a few weeks earlier. In youth hostels in Copenhagen and Amsterdam, we had seen handwritten ads on notice boards from other travellers with cars looking for gas money to take someone to, say, Berlin or Stockholm. There were also ads from women looking for rides, willing to pay the cost of the gas to get there. These were the ads that really interested us. In no time, we made the decision to buy an old used car and see if we could take advantage of these ads. Despite our love of hitchhiking, the thought of jumping into our own car when it was raining, with two damsels at our side, was too hard to resist. Perhaps it was a case of "the grass is always greener on the other side."

12

The Saab

Enjoy the side trips to the fullest. Something more important than the thing you're hunting could be right there by the side of the road.

— Yoshihiro Togashi

O ur plan was to buy a real beater of a car, siphon the gas at night from parked cars and drive to youth hostels to pick up women who would pay us gas money to take them wherever they wanted to go. (At that time in northern Europe, gas cost a fortune and was a significant expense when owning a car.) We would then use their gas money to pay for our hotel, dinner and the bar bill that night, and repeat the next day at our leisure.

I had siphoned gas before and convinced Blair it was easy. You just suck hard on the hose that has one end inserted in the gas tank. The moment the gas starts flowing in the hose, get it out of your mouth in one hell of a hurry and into the spout of a five-gallon container. A great plan. All we needed was a five-foot hose and a jerry can. Once Blair was convinced that we could siphon the gas, he was in on buying a car.

Apparently, the best place in Scandinavia to buy a used car was Gothenburg, Sweden. By a complete fluke, our only pen pal in Scandinavia was in Gothenburg. I have no idea why Gothenburg was great for used cars, but the city was not far away, so off we went the day after we got our money, still hung over from a night on the town. Getting to Gothenburg was easy. We even got there on our dream ride with two young blondes who picked us up.

We easily found the apartment of our pen pal, Anna, and she and her family warmly welcomed us. But immediately, Blair and I saw a problem. Their apartment was not just small, it was tiny. Even the living room was cramped.

Blair immediately pulled me aside and whispered, "Did you tell Anna we were going to stay with her? This place is the size of a closet. Where the hell are we going to sleep? Maybe under the kitchen table? You really screwed up, Jim."

I realized that rolling out our sleeping bags on the living room floor, as we had done in Southampton, would not work with Anna. I looked at Blair, he nodded and we silently agreed to check into the local youth hostel, after taking Anna's family up on their offer for dinner, of course.

The following day, we must have toured all of Gothenburg on foot, with Anna leading the way, including seeing one of the largest amusement parks in Europe. Water seemed everywhere, and the city was terrific, but our minds were really on buying a used car. As we walked and walked, both Blair and I were trying to find a used car lot, but never saw one.

The next day, we scouted on our own all the used car lots in the city, looking for a beater. Our price limit did severely restrict the inventory of cars available. After viewing several lots with nothing available, we ran across a guy who had a 1956 Saab parked at the very back of the lot, with a price the equivalent of

$130. I have forgotten how many kilometres it showed on the speedometer, but it was a lot. The car looked very tired, but the price was right. Blair took it for a spin, and he liked it. I relied on his judgment. It started right away but had an odd noise coming from the engine, something like that of a lawnmower. However, it did seem to go in the direction you pointed it in.

Realizing the sales guy really wanted to get this thing off the lot, we offered the equivalent of about eighty bucks. After some negotiation, Blair and I finally agreed on an amount closer to one hundred dollars. Blair told the salesman that in Canada it was the custom whenever you bought a car that they would throw in a free tank of gas. After a gasp, he agreed, and gave us ten litres of fuel as part of the deal. We had forgotten about insurance but found we could buy just one month of liability insurance for the equivalent of five dollars. We now had a car for just over a hundred dollars, including some gas and insurance.

Excited as hell, Blair drove our new machine to the youth hostel and scanned the ads. We were very happy campers because by chance, two girls were looking to go to Copenhagen the next day. For now, we changed our plans to see the rest of Sweden and agreed to take them to Copenhagen for double the cost of a tank of gas. Things were looking up and would soon get even better.

We drove back to Anna's to show off our new purchase. They were so kind and took us out for dinner to celebrate. We tried to pay a bit but our heart was not in it. They paid the entire bill. When Blair and I left the next morning, we gave them a long thank-you note instead, even throwing in a bit of Swedish to show them how much we appreciated their generosity.

The next morning, we found the girls at the hostel and got an early start. We drove south to the ferry and Copenhagen. But after only a few minutes on the road, I had to come to a sudden stop.

A dapper and proud Blair showing off our new car, a 1956 Saab.

The car behind us could not stop in time, and crashed into our beautiful Saab. This was only the second day we had owned it! Both Blair and I jumped out and screamed at the poor guy who had hit us, showing him all the damage to the trunk of our car. Well, some of it was from before, but it did make a loud noise when he hit us, and there were clearly some fresh dents on the trunk. His bumper was quite damaged and he seemed to feel guilty about the accident, so we quickly settled. We offered a deal: if he immediately gave us the equivalent of forty dollars in cash, we would skip all the insurance claims and paperwork. In a second, he accepted. Now we were really rolling in cash.

After a long day, we took our two unimpressed passengers to their destination, an expensive youth hostel in Copenhagen, even though we were getting a bit low on gas. We wanted to use our funds to pay for our room that night and for dinner at an actual restaurant.

By this time, though, we realized we might have made a slight error. The Saab was powered by a two-cycle engine, something our super salesman had forgotten to tell us. That was why the engine sounded like a lawnmower: it was the exact replica of one you'd find in a mower. That meant we had to add oil to the gas, in a ratio of fifty parts gas to one part oil. So, our siphoning idea had its first hiccup. We not only needed gas but oil as well.

I found a local gas station and bought the smallest oilcan I could find and a small hose. We were now all set for Operation Fill Her Up: siphoning gas from parked cars in the dark. That evening, Blair and I drove around a dimly lit neighbourhood of Copenhagen, looking for a parked car where we could unscrew the gas cap and siphon some gas before the owner discovered our skullduggery. However, it was not easy to find such a car tucked away in the dark. Neither of us wanted to start the sucking thing on the hose due to the fear of swallowing a litre of gas. Then there was the problem of getting caught. We were chickening out fast.

After an hour of driving around, we found a car on a poorly lit street. We tossed a coin and Blair lost. So, out with the hose and the jerry can. Quietly, Blair turned the cover on the gas tank, fed the hose in the tank and started sucking on the hose. I guess he was too enthusiastic or nervous, because very quickly a rush of gas went right into his mouth. He yelled, far too loudly, spat out the gas and ran back to the Saab.

With his lips still dripping with gas, Blair screamed at me, "I am finished with one of your craziest, stupidest ideas ever."

"Sorry, Blair. Sorry. I guess you might be right. Perhaps it wasn't the greatest of ideas after all."

"No kidding," he hollered. "Now it's your turn, since you're the so-called expert on siphoning gas."

Someone must have heard us yelling at each other, as a light went on in the house next to us. It was time to get out of there with Mr. Saab.

I knew now that we were going to have to break down and buy gas. After watching Blair's experience, I certainly was not keen on filling my own mouth with gas. Our plan of paying nothing for gas and then living off the gas money that women would give us was falling apart.

The next day, things got a lot worse. Blair and I wanted to explore Germany and, at some point, get to our pen pal in Berlin. But the only ride-share we saw on the board at the youth hostel was to take someone back up to Norway again, so we skipped it. Instead we headed south, crossing into Germany without a paying customer. After having stopped on the side of the highway, we noticed that the car did not exactly jump to a start when I turned the key. It had that terrible sound of turning over and over, around and around. It did start, but this was a warning that something was wrong.

The exact problem became evident later in the day.

While on the highway, our beloved Saab started dying. It stopped going forward and coasted to a full stop. We let it rest a bit, then luckily got it to start again and into a service station a few kilometres up the road. In a few minutes, the mechanic came back and said, in broken English and German, that the generator was kaput because the battery had no charge at all. He could get a new one, but it was far out of our price range.

After I started having a hissy fit in front of him, the mechanic offered to charge up the battery for next to nothing. We told him we were two lads who had gotten taken by a Swedish salesman. (We hoped, for some reason, that he disliked the Swedish.) At this point, Blair realized that the probability of future repair costs was about 100 percent.

Out of the blue, he said, "I don't want anything to do with the friggin' Saab, and I want out. Not tomorrow, not the next day, but right now."

I didn't know what to say.

"You can keep the damn car," he continued, "but I want my fifty bucks back. That's fair, because it's half the value of the car."

"Look, we got into this thing together, and there's no way you're going to abandon me now."

Blair barked back, "It was never my idea to buy the car in the first place. This goddamn thing could bankrupt us both."

This was the first major fight of our two-month trip. For a short while, it was touch and go whether we would keep travelling together. Almost everyone we met on the road had started off travelling with a buddy but ended up on their own. Often, they had simply decided to go their separate ways after a few weeks. It was always the other guy's fault. But neither of us really wanted to split up, so we worked out a compromise. We would sell the car and split the proceeds. It dawned on me that perhaps it wasn't that Blair wanted to have his fifty bucks back and still have me keep the car. Instead, he truly wanted us to sell the car and hoped that I would quickly come to the same conclusion.

By luck, Blair and I were only 175 kilometres from Luxembourg, where Icelandic Airlines lands in Europe. Hundreds of young travellers took Icelandic Airlines from New York to Luxembourg. It was the cheapest way to get to Europe. We, in turn, would eventually take Icelandic Airlines back to America, leaving from this very spot. Over the years, the arrivals area of the Luxembourg airport had become Europe's largest open market for selling used cars to newly arriving tourists from the United States. Everyone knew about it. There were signs everywhere for used cars for sale, more commonly Volkswagen buses. Those with a lot more money than us would buy or sell used Volkswagen buses from guys just leaving Europe for North America. But we understood that a few beaters like ours would often be in the mix of cars for sale.

We were told that as you got off the plane, car owners — in this case us — would hold up signs, hoping to dump their car. Our advantage was that we could undercut the market with our Saab. Few people, if any, had paid only one hundred dollars for their car. And this was 1964. That meant that a 1956 Saab like ours was only eight or nine years old, even though they must have been a very painful eight years. Our new plan was to get to the airport in Luxembourg, hopefully get the car there as well, sell the car at the airport quickly and split the proceeds.

It seemed like the battery was lasting a maximum of about 150 kilometres before it needed charging, which meant we could almost get to Luxembourg. I really didn't think there was a hope of the car making it all the way. If it did, our prospective buyers might be put off a tad if our car wouldn't start.

Our plan was to drive the car maybe a hundred kilometres, at the most, toward Luxembourg, find a gas station in a small town and get it charged up. On the way, I would drop Blair off at a good place to hitchhike to Luxembourg. He would head to the airport and meet incoming flights with a sign selling our fabulous Saab at a rock-bottom price. Meanwhile, I would hitch from the garage while the car charged and meet him at the airport.

We decided that Blair would ask $275 for the car. As soon as anyone at all interested approached us, Blair would have a story ready. He would say that his partner owned half the car, but he could get him down to $240, as he needed to sell the car today.

Early the next morning, we drove toward Luxembourg. I dropped Blair off at a good hitchhiking spot, and within fifty kilometres of the Luxemburg airport, I was able to find a repair shop while the Saab was still running. I hoped to catch up with him and be at the airport by eleven at the latest. Blair's job was simply to sell the Saab to some naive buyers fresh off the plane.

While at the repair shop, I tried to start the car again, but it could not be revived. It had died. I told the mechanic that since I was coming back with some buyers, it might help if he could somehow solve the generator problem, or at least charge the battery and make sure it started when I got back.

I hitched to the airport, arriving an hour late. Running up to Blair, I yelled at him, "Right after you left me, that damn car would not start again!"

Blair stopped me just as I was about to go on. He had found two Americans fresh off the boat, so to speak, just getting off the plane from New York. They had agreed to buy the Saab for $225 and were standing right beside him.

Initially, I shut up, but then launched into a rehearsed speech. "How could you possibly give the car away like that, right under my nose?" I ranted at Blair.

The two Americans looked shocked. "I told you I wanted three hundred dollars — and that's final. I'm nowhere close to being onside at this price you're offering them. You are giving the car away."

After much yelling, I finally agreed to sell at Blair's price of $225. I hoped this would show our buyers that they were getting a really good deal (and later, that they would forgive us for any future mechanical problems with the Saab).

We decided that Blair would take both buyers with him and hitch back to the town where the car was, a thirty-minute hitchhike. Meanwhile, I would go alone to pick up the car, which would start, hopefully, and drive it to the main square, where we would all meet. The obvious question from our buyers: why didn't you drive the car right to the airport? I told them that since we wanted to make sure the car was reliable, I had dropped it off at a garage and paid a mechanic to give it a going-over. They bought my explanation.

When I arrived at the garage, the mechanic said he had managed to charge the battery and it would start, but he gave the car maybe one hundred kilometres before it would die again. He emphasized that it should be charged overnight. For a permanent solution, he could get his hands on a used generator, but that would take three or four days. That was not in the cards, so I paid him, jumped in the car and drove it to the town square, where Blair was just arriving with our buyers. Perfect timing.

I knew our prospective buyers had seen cars like ours for sale at $500 or more at the airport and thought they were stealing this car from us at $225 (and maybe they were). They were willing to go along with anything.

Now it was time for the test drive. It was going to be dusk in about a half hour. Blair and I wanted to sell Mr. Saab quickly, since we feared we would need to turn the lights on. Then it would soon be over, as the battery would readily die. The Americans loved the car, maybe the price even more. As they drove it around the city, our little Saab really seemed to be on its best behaviour.

Blair sat in the front, with me in the back. He pointed out all of Mr. Saab's little features to our potential buyers, except the radio. He was worried that our buyers might want to turn it on and further deplete the battery. Not certain how much time we had left before the battery ran out of juice, I was a nervous wreck with each minute they drove the car. I figured we still had another thirty minutes before the car would just roll to a permanent stop. We needed to wrap this up quickly. I was also worried because the Americans were suggesting alternate plans.

"We're planning to find a hotel in this small town," said one of them. "All of us could go out to dinner together, then settle the car sale in the morning."

There was no hope that our Saab would be alive in the morning. Without telling Blair, I decided to have another fight with him in front of our purchasers.

"Look, guys," I started in a serious tone, "Blair and I are planning to each go our own way after the sale of this car. And I already made it clear that I wanted my half of the cash tonight. So, I'll tell you what. I'll sell my half at one hundred bucks right now."

At first Blair was really mad, but he caught on quickly, knowing that two hundred dollars was still a lot more than nothing.

He piped up: "I'll agree to that new price only if we can do a deal now, not tomorrow. That way, we can all go our own way tonight." They agreed.

At this point, I jumped into the driver's seat and headed for the nearest bank. It was close to dusk and I noticed that some cars on the road had put their lights on. I knew that if I put the lights on, the battery would fade quickly. In no time, we would grind slowly to a permanent stop, perhaps right in front of the bank. This would not be a good selling feature.

When the Americans asked why I had not turned on the lights, Blair came up with the most memorable line of our trip.

"In Europe, it's the custom not to put your lights on until it's completely dark, so we leave them off like the locals."

Every time I saw a car coming toward us with its lights on, I winced.

The new price still gave us a hundred-dollar profit, less the cost of insurance, the hose, gas, oil and a few big nights out at a pub. We closed the deal, signed some papers and a bill of sale, ran into the bank and cashed their travellers' cheques. All of us then went back to what was now their car. I hoped like hell it would start, and it did. And just like that, they drove out of sight. Blair and I ran to a side street and started hitchhiking in the opposite direction we had told the Americans. We now had an extra two hundred dollars, along with another forty bucks from the accident. We were rich.

I did feel a bit guilty about the Saab sale. On the other hand, I felt a lot better lowering the price to two hundred dollars, knowing they were originally going to pay more. That price differential might compensate, in part, for the cost of a used generator and perhaps many other failed parts in the future. They had paid almost nothing for the Saab, and it was a good deal for them. Well, sort of.

That night, in an undisclosed place, Blair and I found a pub and drank the night away, toasting each other in our newfound freedom without the burden of a car. Having Blair push me to get his fifty bucks back or else sell the car had worked out well. We felt grateful to be back to hitching. We should never have left it. As I sipped my third beer that evening, my hope was that the generator had lasted at least until the next day and our purchasers were not sitting by the side of the road in a lifeless car saying rude things about us. With more cash to complete our trip than we had only two weeks earlier, we decided just to stick to the original plan — whatever that was.

13

Jumping the Wall

A ship in harbour is safe, but that is not why ships are built.
— John A. Shield

We were back to the wonderful advantage of hitch-hiking, which was meeting the people who actually live in a country, not the tourists who were just there for a visit. Once we got a ride, we would answer the standard questions, which were always "Where are you going? Where have you been? Where are you from?"

Our answer to the first question was always "We are going wherever you're going." For example, on our very first ride from the small town near where we sold the Saab, we were picked up within ten minutes by a single driver in a Volkswagen. I sat in the front, Blair in the back with the packs. The conversation from my side went something like this:

"Did you say you were going to Cologne? Yes, that's exactly where we are heading."

Meanwhile, Blair tried to find Cologne on our map to see if it was anywhere close to our route.

"No, we are not from California. We are from western Canada. That's C-A-N-A-D-A."

"Yes, I heard Cologne is the most beautiful city in all of Germany, but I am not sure we have time to spend much time there."

"Yes, modern Germany is indeed beautiful. You have done so much."

At this point, I leaned over to the back seat and whispered to Blair, "Don't mention the war."

And so on. When I sat in the front seat, it was my obligation to carry on the conversation for the entire ride. On our next ride, I would get in the back, and it would become Blair's turn to entertain our new driver.

Just as we had found with European drivers who had given us rides back in Canada, the people who picked us up now were truly proud of their country. They loved to go on and on about why Germany, for example, was far better than France. Then they would talk about some obscure town in Germany and ask if we had been there yet, since it was the best place in their whole nation. We would soon learn the politics of the country, the gossip, the best places to go, etc.

Hitchhiking was fabulous in Germany. Blair and I would rarely wait more than fifteen minutes. When we had, maybe, six to eight rides every single day, we certainly heard a lot of different views on what made the country tick. Looking back, I realize now that it was only about twenty years after the Second World War, so it was still very fresh in the minds of all our drivers. Yet, we would rarely hear a driver talk about the war. It was an undercurrent but never mentioned.

We found the Germans just as efficient and precise as expected. After hitching across North America, Great Britain, Holland, Denmark and Scandinavia, Blair and I were seeing vast differences in the outlook of the people we met, depending on where they were from. Our drivers, almost always a single driver in need of conversation, would often drone on about their future and that of their country, or why they liked accounting, for example.

Now with more money in our hands, we were budgeting about three dollars a day: a 50 percent increase in our standard of living. As a result, when we ended up in a small town in Germany, we could afford to stay in a youth hostel. By 1964, Germany's system of youth hostels was famous. There were hundreds of them scattered across the country, all quite reasonable in cost, though still above our old budget. They were very clean, comfortable and well run. But they had rules. Boy, did they have rules.

Our first stay in a German youth hostel — emphasis on the word *German* — was quite an experience. When you check in, they go over the 350 rules regarding the establishment, including that the door is locked at precisely ten in the evening, and too bad if you don't make it home in time. An employee of the hostel always stood by the door at, say, 9:59 p.m., hoping to lock the door directly in the face of some poor hitchhiker who was five seconds late returning.

Just getting out of the hostel in the morning was sometimes difficult. You had to make your own bed in the morning. It sounds easy, but when Frau Helga came over to inspect our beds, she would rip out the sheets and say they were not even, not tight enough, or the blanket on top was not perfectly square. Again and again I would try to please her. This was just not my skill set. More than four times each morning, I would try to make that bed to her satisfaction. If Helga appeared happy with how you had made the bed, her next test was to bounce a Deutschemark on top of it. If it bounced, this was a good sign that the blankets were correctly tucked in, nice and tight. If the coin just sat there, as it always did with me, she would wave her finger and move on to inspect the bed of some other poor soul. My worry was that I would get trapped in one of these youth hostels for the rest of my life. I would spend all morning trying to make the bed properly, and then at, say, precisely 10:00 a.m., she would go off-shift, only to return the next morning to repeat the process.

Blair and I were hitching our way slowly through small towns to Berlin, where we had yet another pen pal waiting for us. Our plan was to hitchhike through the long corridor that ran through East German territory to the American-controlled side of Berlin, where our pen pal lived with her parents.

To get to Berlin, one had to start in West Germany, with a driver who was going all the way to West Berlin, some 150 kilometres away from the border between West and East Germany. Since the route was entirely in East Germany, one could not stop or be dropped off. We had started our trip early in the morning, worried that the border would be packed with hitchhikers trying to get to Berlin. We were lucky, as no other hitchhikers were there, and soon got a ride from a fellow who lived in the American section of West Berlin and who offered to take us directly to our pen pal's home.

Just before we got to the border, our driver made sure that we didn't have a radio or any Western magazines, because if the guards did search, these items would be confiscated and his trip would be delayed for many hours while the guards combed his car hoping to find more banned items. On the West German side of the border we simply pulled up to a hut, where a British guard examined our passports and waived us on after a few questions. The reception was far more serious as we crawled in heavy traffic to the guard house in East German territory, staffed by Soviet guards. Brandishing firearms, they asked us in German, and in a very serious manner, for our documents. The car was briefly searched, no magazines were found, and it seemed fortunate that we were able to give the guards the address of where we were staying in West Berlin.

Our route was on the former Hannover-to-Berlin autobahn, which was in a state of disrepair compared to the autobahns in West Germany. Indeed the speed limit was only seventy kilometres per hour, due to the condition of the road, about half the speed the large German cars travelled on the autobahns in the West.

I was immediately struck by miles of barbed wire on both sides of the highway, which stretched all the way to Berlin. Also, the overpasses were often full of children, not smiling and waving but just staring at the traffic below. Beyond the barbed wire, the countryside was all a dull grey. A few buildings stood out, but everything looked drab.

East Berlin looking drab and uninviting.
The Wall dominated Berlin. Barbed wire was everywhere.

After making it to West Berlin we were dropped off at the home of our pen pal. We were met at the door of a large apartment by Amelia, our fräulein from Berlin who had answered our letters. She was excited to put Blair and me up for three nights. (Well, it was really her parents who seemed especially pleased to see us.)

West Berlin was surrounded by East Germany and up against East Berlin. We were interested in seeing East Berlin, but as Germans in West Germany, our pen pal and family were prohibited from visiting there. We had heard from other hitchhikers that the only way into East Berlin was through Checkpoint Charlie, the one gate in the American section of Berlin that led to the part of the city controlled by the Soviet Union.

Curious to explore the forbidden, we worked our way through Checkpoint Charlie on our first day in Berlin. The single crossing point for foreigners to get into East Berlin was only a shack. It was no sweat to get through (out), but passing through the Soviet side (in) was unnerving. We had to fill out numerous forms and tell them exactly when we would return to West Berlin and that we would be back by midnight at the latest. Who knows what could have happened if we had missed the deadline? The Soviet-controlled section had armed, uniformed guards staring at us with stern faces wherever we looked, unlike on the American side. There was barbed wire everywhere. This was serious.

Naively, we asked the West Berlin border guard to stamp our passports with the famous, and unofficial, Checkpoint Charlie stamp: a large red circle with the words CHECKPOINT CHARLIE in the middle. It was dated October 7, 1964. At the time, I didn't think anything of it.

We initially spent only half a day in East Berlin. We went back to see more of it a second day but soon returned to the

The famous Checkpoint Charlie stamp in my passport.

West, as there was really nothing to see. The thrill was just in getting there. At that time, West Berlin was an economic miracle, considering the devastation it saw in the war, with bright lights, nightclubs and a high standard of living. East Berlin was grey-toned, with few lights, bleak and boring. It looked like a prison, a collective punishment by the Soviet Union for war crimes committed by the Third Reich on the Eastern Front. No one we met smiled, almost as if smiles were forbidden. The East Berliners were all dressed in drab, colourless clothes. They walked slowly with no social contact. We were fascinated with the contrast between the free and wild West Berlin and the regimented, drab East.

We could see the long, concrete wall between East and West Berlin everywhere. It had been built in 1961 to stop the East Germans defecting to the West in large numbers. The barrier included strategically placed guard towers. Between the wall and the East German buildings was a large space of nothing: forty metres known as the death strip, where the East German border guards shot people trying to escape. The wall, maybe eight feet high, had rolls of barbed wire on the top. On the East German side were lots of towers with soldiers holding machine guns, ready to kill someone who was stupid enough to try to jump the wall from the east side.

In a moment of true stupidity, I decided to run to the wall from the west side and pretend to jump onto the wall. Blair took my picture.

Once back home, I could pretend that I was jumping the wall from the east side and had escaped. At the time, I did not know that the wall was not split exactly on the border between East and West Germany but technically stood five metres into East German territory. So when I touched the wall on the West German side, I was actually in East German territory and could have been shot by one of the trigger-happy East German border guards.

Anyway, it's a great picture.

Me pretending to jump the Wall from the west side, unaware that the ground directly beneath me was actually East German territory.

Blair and I had a wonderful time in West Berlin. Amelia and her family took us to a large beer hall with a live oompah band for dinner and many, many large beers. It was jam-packed. We saw the imposing, neoclassical Brandenburg Gate, built in the late eighteenth century. It was the former city gate of Berlin and one of the most famous landmarks of Germany. On the far side of it lay East Berlin. This gate is where US presidents John F. Kennedy and later Ronald Reagan gave their famous speeches calling for the opening up of East Berlin. We visited the modern downtown and toured many parks and open spaces. I was very impressed with Berlin's progress after the devastating war. It was hard to believe that less than twenty years earlier it had been a war-torn city.

Our pen pal Amelia, her family and me, dressed to the nines and ready for a night out on the town. I don't recall how all six of us were able to fit in the car!

Now with a little more coin, we tried to buy a beer or something for our hosts, but they insisted on paying. Only on the last night did they let us buy them all just a one-litre mug of beer. Everything was big in Berlin. No one ever drank out of a beer glass that was not a full litre in size.

The next morning, after four days in Berlin, we thanked our
pen-pal family for being so kind to us and hitched back to West
Germany with just one ride, just as we had on arrival. They
were an amazing family. I am sure Amelia's parents even took
time off work to spend more time with us. Perhaps they wanted
to show how wonderful Berliners were, so proud of their city
and so changed from the Germany of twenty years ago.

14

Heading South

The gentle reader will never, never know what a consummate ass he can become until he goes abroad.

— *Mark Twain, The Innocents Abroad*

It was fall, getting cold, and our fellow hitchhikers were all heading for the south of France. Paris was first on our list of places to see. I had written to 'The Newspaper' in Paris, but nothing came back. As result, we were forced to stay in one of the city's youth hostels. We soon discovered that Paris was not a place for those with little money. Not only did they ignore us with our far-from-perfect French, but they had absolutely no interest in someone who had no money.

We saw the sights and nursed an espresso in a café for hours, poring over a copy of the *International Herald* I had found on an empty table. Its weekly edition was printed in English and sold on every corner of the world. It was the only newspaper to read. For me, the best thing that came from Paris was the start of my addiction to reading a weekly newspaper from front to back. With my newfound wealth, I either bought or borrowed a copy of this paper every week for the rest of my trip.

The obligatory picture of the Eiffel Tower.

Overall, Paris was not a hit with us. The locals hated us, and everything from a coffee to a meal was far too expensive. After only three days, we both wanted to get the hell out of there, but leaving Paris was not as easy as it should have been. The hitchhiking in France was horrible. At first, Blair and I were happy when a car slowed down, thinking they were going to give us a lift. Instead they just gave us the finger and sped off. We guessed they might have thought we were American, so we put Blair's pack with its prominent Canadian flag out front. However, we soon learned that no matter what we did, it made absolutely no difference. The hitching was just bad.

We often waited two hours for a ride, compared to ten minutes in Germany. The cars that finally picked us up were on the poor side of the equation. When we saw a nice car come around a corner heading for us, we just gave up, as we knew the chances of them picking us up were nil. We even moved off the side of the road in case they were aiming directly at us.

It took us almost three days of constant hitchhiking to make it down to Nice, a distance of about one thousand kilometres. Even though there was a monster freeway all the way down, we wanted to see the country and took the local highways instead. Unfortunately, this turned out to be probably the worst hitchhiking of the trip so far, but at least we made it there safely. Most cars would speed up as they approached us to show their disapproval of what they termed "hippies" on the side of the road, trying to get something for free.

On the other hand, we were amazed at the proportion of rides received from university students who drove twice the speed limit, giving us their opinion on some obscure part of French politics in the south. The contrast between this part of France (Provence) and Paris was amazing. It was like two separate countries. Those who picked us up were far friendlier and very expressive in their speech compared to their countrymen in Paris. They were genuinely interested in our views of the world and, more importantly, of southern France. We were already far happier in southern France than in Paris.

At that time, one would see these small Citroëns throughout France. They had canvas seats and side windows on hinges that one could simply flip open with a hand. The back was one big canvas seat. They were probably the cheapest cars made in all of Europe. These cars were all driven by twenty- to thirty-year-old revolutionaries, with a Gauloise cigarette in their mouth, talking in rapid-fire French while gesturing with their hand to avoid touching the steering wheel. If the driver did touch the steering wheel, it was by accident. The cigarettes were famous. They had no filters, were strong as hell, and rumour had it that the tobacco came from Syria. The first time I tried one, I passed out.

Rides in these Citroëns were probably the most entertaining of our entire trip. Every time Blair and I saw one of them heading our way, there was a reasonable chance they would stop for us. But an issue was just fitting into these cars. They were very small. Because we had two big packs, we would do our common routine — hide one of the packs, perhaps in a ditch, and bring it out of hiding only when one of these Citroëns stopped. Blair and I would flip a coin to see who got the luxurious canvas front seat and who got to squeeze in with the packs in the back. To many a skeptical driver, we had to prove that two packs and a person would indeed fit.

The youth hostel in Nice was full of people we had met on the road and in towns farther north. Like us, all were heading to the warmth of southern France. After a lot of planning of our route in Europe, it had somehow escaped us that it might get cold in the fall on this continent. Our original thought was to spend more time in Austria and Switzerland, but now it was the start of November. We needed warmth, not scenery.

Nice was really two cities. The newer French Quarter had wide boulevards and magnificent buildings, including the opulent five-star Hotel Le Negresco at the end of the Avenue Anglais, the main boulevard along the ocean. But for Blair and me, the best part of Nice was the old walled city, where everyone we knew hung out. The old city had been Greek for thousands of years and, of course, Italian for hundreds of years as well. It was close to the beach, which was not sand but millions of small pebbles. The old walled city was covered in cheap outdoor restaurants and bars. No cars were allowed. If we were not on the beach, we were wandering the old city with the many fellow hitchhikers we had met along the way.

The author in Nice with a bottle of wine purchased at less than the cost of the baguette, roughly the equivalent of twenty cents per bottle.

The price of wine worked in our favour too. Once we had figured out who sold the cheapest wine — who cares about taste? — we bought in volume. Blair and I put a deposit down on a five-litre jug enclosed in straw with large handles on each side. Since each vat was marked with a price for five litres, which was cheaper than buying a litre, we took our five-litre jug and filled it up with red wine from the cheapest vat in town. With our cups from the youth hostel, we each grabbed one of the handles of the jug and walked down the hill to the beach to join our fellow hitchhikers.

Sitting in groups on the edge of the ocean were maybe thirty other hitchhikers, mostly from California, also drinking wine from five-litre jugs. It turned out to be quite a party. By the time noon rolled along, conversations were flowing just like the wine. Lunch and dinners were made up of the best bread I have ever tasted in my life and a large chunk of cheese. Everyone knew where to buy the best bread and the cheapest cheese. We did celebrate one night with ten of us going to an outdoor restaurant in the old city, where one of the guys had arranged with the owner for a cheap meal. The owner even let us bring in our own jugs of wine to hide under our table. As we were in Nice, we all started with a *salade niçoise* and then plates and plates of fish with hot, salted French fries.

The best part about this gang was that they had been everywhere. Most seemed to be going farther south to Spain, since it was even warmer. Some were going to a special colony in Spain where you could grab a room for a buck and be right on an empty white-sand beach stretching for miles. The colony was halfway down the coast of Spain and run by a hippy from California. Some were going in the other direction, heading to southern Italy to escape the cold. We got tips of where to stay and where to go from everyone.

Our original plan was to hang around Spain and then head for Italy and Greece to wait out the winter. Blair and I then started hearing about how great and inexpensive Morocco was. One fellow who had hitched his way back from Morocco and was now on his way to Rome talked about living there for less than two dollars a day and how friendly the people were.

Another hitchhiker said we had to go to Gibraltar and eat in a famous café called Smoky Joe's, owned by an eccentric guy from England. Everyone went there. Apparently, he would stamp your passport, and it was a badge of honour around the world that you had been to his restaurant.

After two days of drinking all day, Blair and I decided to change our route and hitch to Casa Campello, the hippie colony, then on to the cheap and intriguing country of Morocco. We were not sure where to go from there, but one guy who was with us in Nice said that he planned to hitch all the way to Cairo from Morocco, escaping the winter, then hitch back up to Europe from Cairo for the next summer. This route seemed like a great idea. By five, after drinking all day, everything seemed like a great idea.

Nice was the first place where we came across draft dodgers. This was the fall of 1964, and US involvement in the Vietnam War was starting to heat up. The war was always in the news. These guys we met were all from California and had a deferral from the draft of four years while they went to university. But the second they graduated, they were eligible to have their number picked. If that happened, they would be asked to report to a government office to sign up for the US Army.

I listened to these guys into the night, and they explained to me that they were not army deserters. Instead, they were dodging the draft — hence the term *draft dodger*. Most knew that at some point their luck would run out and they would receive a letter from the draft board asking them to report and be inducted into the army. To them, it was important to get out of the United States before that letter arrived. Where better to go than southern France? They didn't want to waste their life by being killed in Vietnam. They knew a lot about the war and explained that in their view, the US was backing the wrong side, the corrupt side of dictators in Saigon that didn't care about the people in South Vietnam. On the other hand, the army and regime of North Vietnam were volunteer-driven, they said, and fighting based on their true beliefs.

In the US, the media and conservative politicians painted the war as dreaded communism versus the free people of South Vietnam living the capitalist way. They sold the war as the last chance to stop communism and its 'domino effect' should the regime of South Vietnam fall. It wasn't hard to be on the draft dodgers' side. Why be shipped to some jungle eight thousand miles away to be ordered to fight and shoot some guy who had volunteered to fight for his country? It would be a year before the massive anti-war protests started on US campuses. Little news was coming back from Vietnam, but these draft dodgers made the point that a lot more was happening than the public knew, and none of it was good. I didn't believe it at the time, but as we kept travelling and talking to more draft dodgers, I realized this was not an exaggeration and became sympathetic to their cause.

I realized that if I had been born in the US, I too might have left the country to avoid the war. I probably would have done all I could to avoid having my name come up; I would have gone to graduate school, then gotten some sort of PhD or even developed bone spurs. For sure, I would not have gotten on that plane heading for Vietnam. These guys had a lot of guts to leave the US and wait until the madness was over. One might be inclined to do what one's parents said was the right thing to do, since most of the country supported the war at that time. It was not an easy decision, and it's hard to say what I would have done if I had walked in their shoes.

We started to notice that people didn't ask us where we were from anymore. Instead, they tried to guess what Californian city we were from. The usual question was "Are you from LA or San Francisco?" Whatever the reason, a vast number of hitch-hikers were from the western US and Australia, and only the rare traveller was from Boston or New York. Meanwhile, the West Coast of Canada, despite having only 10 percent of the nation's population, produced about half of the Canadian hitchhikers we encountered. It seemed that if you were from the West Coast of North America, you had a good chance of sitting on a beach in Nice with your fellow hitchhikers in the fall of '64. I figured that for those growing up on the West Coast, there must be more freedom to choose your own lifestyle without the same drive to succeed and make money that you find on the East Coast.

After three days of drinking, Blair and I varied our plan a little from the previous day. We thought we would join a small group of hitchhikers heading for 'heaven', some 1,500 kilometres southwest along the coast of Spain. After stopping in Gibraltar, we would head on to Morocco.

Everyone complained about the hitchhiking in France compared to Germany. However true, the laid-back lifestyle and lack of regimentation in France were more suited to me than strict Germany, so I just put up with the poor hitching. Casa Campello really did sound wonderful. All we had to do was get there. It meant hitchhiking across southern France to the border of Spain, then halfway down the coast of Spain.

Unfortunately, the hitchhiking in Spain was reported to be even worse than in France.

15

Gun-Toting Annie

*At age twenty-two I set what I insist is an all-time record for
distance hitchhiking in Bermuda shorts: 3,700 miles in three weeks.*

— Hunter S. Thompson

On a warm day in Nice with not a cloud in the sky,
our trip started off well. We got a ride after waiting
only an hour, which was outstanding for France. Our
starting point had already been scouted out the previous day.
We were going to stand and hitch just past a large roundabout
where the traffic from Nice separated into those heading north
and those heading west along the coast in our direction.

Our first ride took us to a great spot, a hundred kilometres
west of Nice, at an intersection where a local road met the main
highway across southern France. But unfortunately a small
problem arose: two hitchhikers were already standing there.

A hitchhiker's etiquette prevails when it comes to these
situations, which happens in countries where hitching is bad.
The worst thing you can do is simply walk three hundred metres
or so ahead of the others and start hitching, getting first crack
at all the possible cars coming down the road. If you do this,

you can expect a screaming match or worse, especially if they have been waiting hours for a ride. The next worst thing is to walk just past them and start hitchhiking. Drivers don't like to see groups on the road and will worry that all the hitchhikers are together. They fear that if they stop, they might be swarmed.

Therefore, we would walk by the hitchhikers, toward our destination, and find a reasonable place out of their sight, maybe half a kilometre down the road. We would often see our rivals going by later in a car, having gotten a ride, and they would wave to us. Their spot, of course, was now free, and we would walk back to where they were, the best possible spot to get a ride. The other reason not to interfere with others' hitching is that one always seems to bump into the same people along the way. We were often welcomed by hitchhikers whom we had been nice to and whose spot we hadn't stolen. It would have been a far different reception if we had taken their place on the road.

Slowly, Blair and I worked our way across southern France, with most of the rides being short. Cars that picked us up were often beat-up and small, while the large Mercedes would speed up as they passed us. This was not encouraging, as we knew the hitching would get worse once we crossed the border to Spain.

Our goal, Casa Campello, was in front of us, and we hitchhiked from morning to night to reach the potential haven as soon as we could.

Finally crossing the border of Spain, we were dropped off at one intersection where we waited endlessly for a ride. It must have been a very long stop for other hitchhikers before us: on a signpost on the side of the road some hitchhiker had written, "Day 12 — We killed Dave yesterday and ate him." Thankfully, we didn't have to wait twelve days for a ride. And I had no thoughts of eating Blair.

The author getting a tad lazy after a few hours of hitchhiking
without luck near the French and Spanish border.

After several hours, we finally got lucky. At a fork in the
road, a car stopped and out came a woman whose name was
Annie. She had only arrived in Spain a few days earlier and
was hitching alone down the coast to Gibraltar. Hitching as
a single woman in Spain meant you got picked up by every
second car. Our odds were about one hundred times worse. Of
course, there were significant dangers for a woman hitchhiking
alone. Somehow, she had to rely on second sense, judging
whether the person picking her up was okay. For that and many
other reasons, most single women joined up with a guy, another
woman or two guys for safety.

In Spain, three people hitching, with one a woman, was far
superior to just two guys. The odds improved when one of the
guys hid on the side of the road with his pack. We convinced
Annie to join us. Within fifteen minutes, a car stopped with
lots of room, and all three of us got a long ride to a small town.
Without her, my guess is that we would have waited two or

three hours at that spot. We promptly nabbed another long ride to a small village right on the sea.

The village looked like a perfect place to stop for the night, so we found a single room in a cheap hotel for the three of us. Annie was quite a character. She talked non-stop, pausing only to breathe. She'd then look at us for comment. For example, Annie once claimed that her country, the good old USA, would soon invade Canada. It was just a matter of time. Nothing could save us. Unless Blair or I jumped in within two seconds, she was on again about some other topic that was bugging her. Some of what she said made sense, but most did not. Annie certainly filled the gaps in conversations between Blair and me.

After a nice dinner in the hotel, we bought two bottles of wine and brought them back to our room. It seemed that Annie had about thirty small bottles of hard liquor in her pack. Each was about two ounces, similar to those you would find on an airplane. Somehow, she had charmed a steward on the flight coming over, and he had given her these bottles on the plane as a parting gift.

Blair decided to fortify our drinks by pouring a two-ounce bottle of Scotch, rye or gin into our glasses already filled with wine. After a number of these concoctions, all three of us passed out on top of the bed, fully clothed. Annie still had her high leather boots on.

Early in the morning, with all three of us on top of the covers, I thought I heard someone screaming. It was Annie.

"Someone just touched me. I know it. I felt it twice. You don't know, but I have a gun in my boots. One false move, guys, and I will blow your feet off. I am not bloody kidding!"

The gun comments truly woke me up, and I leaned away from Annie. Despite the commotion, Blair was still snoring, oblivious to her accusations. I thought that maybe with Blair still sleeping and unable to defend himself, I should report him as the guilty one.

There was no way either of us had touched her like she claimed, unless Blair had moved his foot while sleeping. Finally, he woke up in a start and we both jumped out of bed at the same time, our heads pounding from the previous night.

Our plan had been to hitchhike with Annie all the way to our destination, but that was not going to happen now. She got up quickly, snarled again at us, gathered every one of her tiny liquor bottles and left the room in a huff to hit the road. Blair and I were both really hung over, so we just went back to bed and closed our tired eyes until it was time to check out.

Once again, it was just the two of us hitching. But luck was with us, and in an hour we got a nice ride in the direction we wanted. We were close now to our goal, this perfect resort on the sea, which in our minds grew better and better as time went on.

Casa Campello was near Alicante, a large city about halfway down the coast of Spain. At last, after a full day of hitching, there it was in front of us, only thirty feet from a kilometre-long white beach in the middle of nowhere. There was a small general store nearby where we could buy beer, wine and groceries, and an open bar and restaurant at the hotel, which we could barely afford. The rooms were cheap and basic, with two old beds crammed into a ten-foot-square space. The view from the room was out of this world, however, as the units were only a few feet from a wide open beach and the sea. We knew about a quarter of the people there, but the place had a major flaw. It had three times as many guys as women. A poor ratio but one I was getting used to in hitching, since few women hitched in Spain. Those who did were usually with their boyfriends.

We spent our days there getting up around eleven, swimming, drinking and eating a large dinner at ten or eleven in the evening or later, then staying up most of the night, drinking cheap wine and beer on the beach. The stories we heard were from a very well-travelled group of about thirty hitchhikers, all with little money and high spirits.

By this time, Blair and I had been travelling together for many months. After a while, certain small things about someone become annoying, which are magnified when you are together twenty-four hours a day. We had both grown up in families where gourmet cooking was not exactly the norm. In fact, my father's last words to me as I left for university were "Always order your meat well done." Whenever we had a chance to cook, I used to cook our meat until it looked like a black hockey puck, and to Blair, I had ruined the meal.

Though there was a restaurant nearby, we tended to cook our own dinners, often eating in groups. The place had an out-door kitchen of sorts, consisting of a few hot plates and some old pots, pans and utensils. One night, we bought a can of spaghetti sauce that was probably a year old and some freshly made pasta from the local store. Being only a few feet from the sea, we decided to just boil the pasta in sea water. What could go wrong?

Throughout our trip, I had noticed that before Blair even tasted his meal, he always took a salt shaker and doused his food in salt. Regardless of how much salt the chef may have already used in preparing the meal, Blair attacked it with salt. What could I say? Blair liked salt, and here was an easy source of salt water just a few feet away. The pasta looked great as it came out of the pot filled with sea water. As per usual, Blair grabbed a salt shaker and salted our pasta dinner with its sauce before even tasting it.

I tried one bite and gagged. The overall taste of our dinner was salt. You couldn't taste the sauce or the pasta, just salt. We tried smothering our pasta with more sauce, but it didn't work.

We were eating what I would call a plate of salt. I couldn't stop laughing, and of course, later that night I told everyone I knew the story of Blair and his love of salt.

Months earlier, Blair had noticed that I ate my dinners very slowly, whereas he would gulp his food down as if we were in a competition to see who could be the fastest. Perhaps my slowness went back to my mother's words as she had towered over me as a child: "Now, Jimmy, chew all of your meat slowly and finish those peas. Don't rush. Eat slowly. Lay your fork down. Don't hold your knife in your hand while you eat. Will you ever learn?"

We were lucky that we were such close friends and could tolerate each other's faults.

16

Smoky Joe's

Actually, the best gift you could have given her was a lifetime of adventures.

— attributed to Lewis Carroll

I had a small problem. Besides still being a tad smelly, I had two large holes in the bottom of my shoes. They were not going to last long. Earlier, I had asked my mother to buy some shoes and send them to Berlin, and if they didn't arrive there, then onto Nice poste restante. But since they had not arrived, I asked my mother to have them forwarded to Madrid, where we were headed. But after our horrible hitchhiking in Spain, Blair was not keen to leave this little bit of paradise at Casa Campello to stand on the road for days just so I could get my shoes. It was a real long shot the shoes were even there. I couldn't blame him. If the situation were reversed, I would have felt the same way.

After five days of doing nothing, I decided to hitch up to Madrid the next day, alone, to check on the post office. Blair would stay by himself for a couple of days here in heaven, then hitch down to Gibraltar. We would meet in four days at either Smoky Joe's, the famous bar-restaurant on the main street in

Gibraltar, or at the youth hostel. I figured it would take a day to get up to Madrid, where I would spend two nights, pick up or buy a pair of shoes, look around the city, then spend about two days hitching to Gibraltar.

I left Blair sleeping, pulled myself out of bed and onto the edge of the highway and started hitching. From Alicante, the large city near Casa Campello, a major highway went straight to Madrid. Just like in France, where all roads led to Paris, in Spain, all roads led to Madrid. Perhaps it was because I was on my own and better looking than Blair, but I was getting rides in the right direction at a relatively fast pace and made it to Madrid that evening.

When I got to the Palacio de Comunicaciones (post office) the next morning, there were no shoes. No package from Mom. I had approached the wicket hoping for shoes but realized this was the third forwarding address for them. Chances were slim of finding them here. I expected a letter from home at least, but there was nothing. Alone for the first time on our trip, I felt truly down as I stepped out of the post office and walked away aimlessly.

By now, my existing shoes had completely fallen apart. It was time to buy another pair. After a lot of exploring Madrid, I found a few stores on the edge of the market that sold used shoes at low prices. Some of these pairs looked brand new. I was not interested in fashionable shoes and couldn't care less about the colour. All I wanted was a sturdy, boot-like pair that would never wear out. I settled on a bright burgundy pair that was a tad bulky. Very la-di-da. I got a great deal, and they even fit.

Granada, a city worth seeing, was on the way to 'Gib', as the Spanish called Gibraltar, but hitching away from Madrid was not as easy as heading toward it. It took most of the day to get to Granada. My goal was to tour the giant Moorish palace, the Alhambra, on a hill overlooking Granada. The palace, which was really a fortress, was built six hundred years ago and was in excellent shape. It was well worth the visit, but I kept thinking that Blair should have been with me. This was far more educational than wasting his time lying on the beach, drinking beer and striking out with girls.

Early the next evening, I arrived in Gibraltar and went directly to the youth hostel. Blair had indeed checked in but was nowhere to be found. Eventually, I found him at Smoky Joe's, the restaurant run by this wild British guy who greeted everyone by name and served a cheap English breakfast with a pint of lukewarm beer. Beans, grilled tomatoes, sausages, fried eggs and a beer. Breakfast turned into dinner, and as the day wore on, the place got louder and louder.

It was quite a crowd. Although hitchhikers dominated, English army cadets working on what they called 'the rock' were all over the place. We knew many of the hitchhikers from our travels. There were also well dressed 'yachties' (sailing types) who had heard of Smoky Joe's as a must-go. With sawdust on the floor, tables jammed everywhere and no room for the servers to walk, the place was not exactly classy. Every liquid came in a one-pint mug, including tea. Most of the mugs looked like they were washed in the morning and then just recycled. The best thing for us was that the food and beer were cheap. It was always full until Joe shut the place down late at night.

Blair and I greeted each other like lost souls, even though it had been only four days. He had arrived a day early, as he had been getting a bit bored at our beach heaven. We spent the night nursing two warm beers and listening to fellow hitchhikers talk about Morocco and Tangier.

Gibraltar was different: a little bit of England sitting in the middle of a dry and desolate landscape. It was comforting to hear English from the locals; it had been months since we left Great Britain. After a few weeks of Spain, it seemed so out of place. 'The rock' was a prized strategic piece of land, as it controlled the strait below it, but since it lacked fresh water and fertile soil, only the surrounding area was inhabited. Legend has it that the Moors first settled Gibraltar in the fourteenth century, only to have it integrated into Spanish territory toward the end of the Reconquest, at the end of the fifteenth century. In 1713 it was ceded to the British. Today, some 250 years later, it remains a British Overseas Territory.

Long ago, a British soldier wrote in his diary, "Here is nothing to do nor any news, all things being dormant and in suspense, with the harmless diversions of drinking, dancing, revelling, whoring, gaming and other innocent debaucheries to pass the time — and really, to speak my own opinion, I think and believe that Sodom and Gomorrah were not half so wicked and profane as this worthless city and garrison of Gibraltar."

Blair and I toured all of Gib. It didn't take long to climb to the top of the rock, a highlight, though I had to be very careful because of my fear of heights. Hundreds of wild monkeys were crawling all over the rock, looking for food from people like us. The view across the strait was spectacular. We could see the North African coast, perhaps only fifteen kilometres away, separated by the deep blue water of the strait. One could only imagine what this place must have been like during the Second World War. Looking down at the water, I could just imagine a German U-boat creeping through the strait. It was easy to see why this rock had been so strategic for so many years.

• • •

We heard that Joe had designed a special stamp for people who wanted to show off that they had been to his restaurant. Just like at Checkpoint Charlie, we got his unique stamp in our passports, stamped by Joe himself. Little did we realize that later on our trip, border guards in North Africa would tell us that these unofficial stamps made our passports void and that therefore we could not enter their country.

At Smoky Joe's we met a few others who were considering hitchhiking across North Africa. It seemed everyone went the same way: counter-clockwise, starting in Gibraltar, down to Marrakesh (which got rave reviews), then up to Fez and across to the border with Algeria. There was some doubt about whether that border was actually open,

The official stamp of Smoky Joe Eating House in Gibraltar, stamped directly onto our passports by Smoky Joe himself.

but most people thought it was if one had the proper visa. It was now mid-November and we figured we could get to Egypt by the end of the year.

There were two advantages to this plan. First, North Africa was about half the price of Europe, and second, it was warmer than Europe. The disadvantage was that we had heard that the hitching was 'challenging', in a word. Regardless, this seemed to be such an adventure that by the time Blair and I left Gibraltar, we had made the call to hitch to Egypt and then see how we could get up to Greece to see our beautiful pen pals.

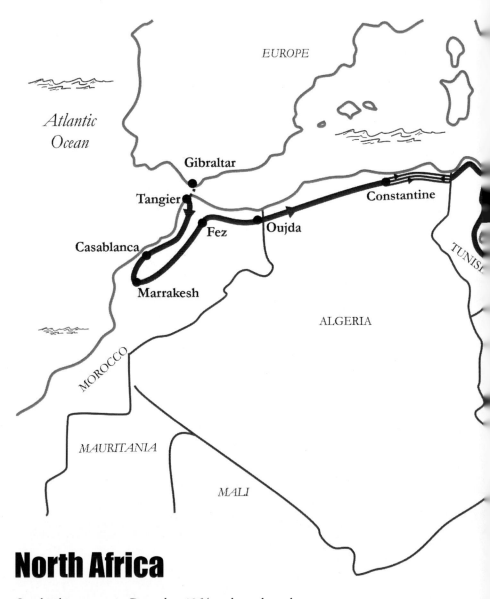

North Africa

Our hitching route in December 1964 took us through the major cities of Morocco, the newly liberated country of Algeria and on to Cairo, Egypt. We booked two third-class train tickets from Cairo to Luxor along the Nile River at two dollars apiece, followed by passage aboard a boat to Beirut, the only available means of reaching the Middle East at that time.

17

Tangier

The real voyage of discovery consists not in seeing new landscapes, but in having new eyes.

— Marcel Proust

The traditional way to Morocco was to take the short ferry across from Gibraltar to Tangier. The problem was that it was expensive — well over three dollars each. The cheapest way to get out of Gibraltar was to hitch to the grubby port town of Algeciras in Spain. A ferry across the strait went to another Spanish town called Ceuta, which was situated in a very small area of maybe fifty square kilometres of North Africa. It was Spanish territory right on the sea. From Ceuta, you hitched to Tangier. The cost of this route was only a dollar, less than a third of the cost of a direct ferry to Tangier. Blair and I had no clue that a small bit of Spain was cut out of the tip of North Africa, but we loved the idea of saving some money.

The ferry was small, like an open barge, with a few cars thrown in for good measure. On the ferry were a couple of other hitchhikers. We were all stuffed in with at least fifty local Arab workers, who commuted every day from North Africa to

Spain, where the wages were far higher. From Ceuta, it was just a short hitch for us to Tangier.

I had taken a lot of notes from our talks with fellow hitch-hikers in Gibraltar. For one thing, we were told to never change our money at a bank in Morocco because the black-market rate was about 50 percent better than what we would get at a bank. This meant we should always go to a money-changer and cash in our travellers' cheques, using the free-floating black-market rate rather than the artificial, propped-up rate given at a bank. We also got addresses and names of places to stay in Tangier, Casablanca, Marrakesh and Fez, and where to eat in each of these cities.

Tangier, at this time, was part of Morocco. It had been a wild, global city prior to 1956, when it joined the Kingdom of Morocco, though it still retained all the features of an international city. This meant there were few taxes, duty-free imports and exports for everything, few rules and little governance. With so few regulations, it attracted a diverse group of characters and a lawless atmosphere. It also became a party town, one of the wildest cities in the world. Countless times, we had been warned to be careful to avoid being taken for all the money we had.

I had been given the name of a small hotel that promised to be clean and one of the cheapest in the city, where a lot of hitchhikers on the circuit stayed. A room for two could be had for the equivalent of less than a dollar. Although I had the name of the hotel written in French, every sign was written in Arabic, which meant we didn't have a hope of deciphering where our hotel was. Blair and I walked into the medina, or old city, made up of many interconnecting small alleys, all twisting around in circles. Large stone walls, apparently from a fifteenth-century Portuguese fortress, surrounded the medina. No cars were allowed in. Everything happened in the medina, despite its maze-like layout. Which way to turn? We were stuck trying to figure out where our hotel was.

After we walked a hundred metres into the medina, we were lost, then swarmed by a number of twelve-year-old kids who spoke excellent English. I asked one of them to help us find the hotel recommended to us and gave him the name in French. He apparently knew the hotel and off we went. The route involved countless turns, twists and alleyways that were no more than three metres wide. Finally, we arrived at the hotel and he marched us up to the 'lobby' (desk). Our young guide demanded baksheesh (money) for taking us to our hotel. From this point on, for our entire trip through Muslim counties, we heard the word *baksheesh* from young kids everywhere. It was slang for "Give us money."

The name of the hotel was in Arabic. I didn't see the French name of the hotel anywhere. Something smelled fishy The boys all seemed way too eager to get us checked in for the five or six nights we were going to stay in Tangier. When I asked the guy behind the desk whether this was the same hotel as the one whose name I had in French, he replied, in broken English, "Yes, sir, of course it is. You are so lucky to have found my hotel. It is the finest hotel in all of Tangier."

The problem was that unlike normal guests, we would have to prepay for our rooms before we were allowed to check in, and that was a considerable sum for us. If we had the wrong hotel, there was no chance of a refund. Luckily, Blair asked to see the French name of their hotel. The manager stumbled. Finally, we figured out that our golden twelve-year-old guide had taken us to a hotel where he would get a kickback, as well as money from us. My hunch had been right. It was not the hotel we wanted. Far from it. Blair and I stormed back down the stairs into the middle of the medina to fume. We were no better off than before, and now surrounded by a new group of twelve-year-olds.

This was not going well. We kept walking, trying to make our way back to the main square where we had started. But it was hopeless in the medina because we felt completely disoriented in the narrow alleys that spilled out everywhere, each one going off in a different direction and never in a straight line. Keeping us confined and disoriented in this maze were the high, ever-present stone walls, like a prison.

By a complete fluke, lost in the middle of the medina, we ran across a fellow hitchhiker we had met in Nice, who knew the hotel we were looking for. He and his friends had considered two hotels in Tangier, and that was one of them. But they were not staying there because they thought the other one was nicer, though a bit more expensive. For us, the golden rule was always to choose the cheapest hotel. *Nicer* never entered into the equation. He took us to the hotel we wanted, and it looked just fine. Blair and I splurged a bit, taking a double room (rather than a triple, which would have meant a mystery roommate).

This was one hell of a city, famous for attracting wealthy gay people, even wealthier partiers, and members of rock bands like the Rolling Stones. They all hung out in Tangier. The smells of the city — spices, sweet tea and cigarette smoke — smothered the air and were with us all the time. The constant noise from the street also never stopped. There was no escape.

And everyone was after money. We kept ours safely in our respective bags, tied to our belt loops. Despite that, I must have felt that bag ten times every minute I was out on the streets. On our first day in Tangier, we found out that every expat living in the city exchanged their money with a money-changer. They all avoided the banks due to the outrageous government exchange rate, about four dirhams to the dollar, compared to six from a money-changer. A huge difference. Out of fear and because Tangier was so cheap, most tourists, who were not part of the hitchhiking crowd, simply went to the bank to change their money into dirhams and were happy campers. Not us.

One of the first scams we heard about in Tangier was a money-changer who worked with the police. He would induce an unsuspecting tourist by giving a slightly better rate than any of the other money-changers, but as soon as the transaction got underway and the tourist signed over a traveller's cheque to him, the police would arrive. There would be a yelling match, with the police saying the tourist must go to jail for illegal money-changing. The money-changer would moan away, pleading the tourist's case with the police, begging them not to shut him down, all in French so that you could partially understand what he was saying. The money-changer would then appear very sincere, saying that these were such nice people (though he had just met them five minutes ago), and rather than have them go to jail, perhaps a fine would suffice. The police would say they'd think about it and suggest a fine of, say, the equivalent of $100 each, or $200 if you looked like a normal tourist. The money-changer would bargain the police down to, say, a $75 fine. At this point, most suckers would gladly pay the fine to avoid spending time in a jail in Tangier. If they were really new to the city, they thought themselves lucky to have met such a nice money-changer who had kept them out of jail and cut their fine in half.

Of course, as soon as they walked away, the police would share half the fine with the money-changer. It was a great scam. To us, even a fifty-dollar fine would set back our trip by weeks. We couldn't afford to be caught in such a scam, but we also could not afford to change our money at the artificial rate charged by the banks. Luckily, most of the money-changers in Tangiers were honest and not into scams. They competed with each other and knew one another well. We just had to find an honest one and understand that they were smarter than us at this game. We needed to be very careful to get the best rate, and even more careful to get the exact amount in dirhams that we had bargained for. Most tourists were short-changed because they were not familiar with the currency.

An expat friend of our hotel manager gave us the location of a fair and honest money-changer, along with the name of a person that we could safely buy hashish from. Blair and I were told the going rate on the black market was about 6.1 dirhams to the dollar. At first, we were offered 5.9 dirhams to the dollar: a helluva lot better than the bank rate of 4 dirhams to the dollar, but still not 6.1. It took us at least ten minutes to get these guys up to the proper rate.

Where to change money and buy hashish might be the two most important contacts in Tangier. Buying hashish was subject to exactly the same scam as changing money. The seller worked with the police to find his suckers, then they would go through the jail-time-fine-cut-the-fine-in-half routine. Almost every twelve-year-old in the medina would ask if we needed to change money or buy hashish, since they could make a lot off the scam, getting a large kickback.

Hashish was cheap. You could fill a small matchbox for a couple of dollars at most, which would last Blair and me most of our time in Morocco. We found our reliable friend's dealer and after getting some local currency, quickly bought our first hash. The next step was to buy a small, thin wooden pipe and a clay cup, about half an inch square, to attach to the end of the pipe. One would simply put the hash in the cup, light it and voila. This was a great experiment for Blair and me, as we had never smoked marijuana in our lives and hash was a step up. We had only been in Tangier for less than six hours and we already had life's essentials.

On the second day, we ran across four California draft dodgers a few years older than us who had been living in the city for a couple of months. They invited us over to their place after dinner to smoke some hashish and learn about Tangier. We entered a small, dark room full of smoke and cushions everywhere. The six of us kneeled around a low table filled with hashish and a number of bowls of fresh tomatoes, of all things. We would smoke their hash, have some tomatoes, then learn from them just how wild this city was and how you really had to watch yourself as newcomers. There were many ways you could get taken. It was really survival of the fittest.

By far, Tangier was the craziest place that Blair and I had ever been. All of our survival experience gained over the last months of hitching was put to the test. If we had just arrived there without going through the learning experiences of the previous few months, we would not have lasted six hours. We would have wound up broke, taken in by various scams by the young but very clever and devious thieves that surrounded us wherever we went. As for hashish, it just put Blair and me into a very sleepy mood. This proved a bit disappointing, but I did like the resulting feeling of total relaxation and being very mellow.

These Californians were similar to the draft dodgers Blair and I had met in Nice. They were all sincere and smart. The bottom line was they didn't want to get killed fighting in a war they didn't support. Recently, North Vietnam had supposedly shot at and torpedoed an American destroyer in the Gulf of Tonkin, although there were no US casualties. This had the effect of ramping up the war significantly.

Everywhere we went, Blair and I were asked our views on Vietnam. Like anything political, it was best to mumble something and move on, even though by now I was firmly against that war. Looking back, I realize now that the news I had swallowed back in Canada was biased and not truthful. Every young person we met was against the war. It was hard to see why the US would not just retreat from the war, move on and let the people of Vietnam decide their own government.

Our days in Tangier started around eleven o'clock in the morning. We would be out smoking and talking with fellow hitchhikers or draft dodgers or many of the very interesting expats that hung around the city. Since we were two young guys travelling together, some people mistakenly thought we were gay, and we were invited to countless gay parties with abundant hash. We walked out of the first party after a few minutes, explaining to our host that we had misunderstood, but they persuaded us to stay. We learned a lot about the expat community in Tangier, which seemed to have a high proportion of gay men. One could live cheaply, the weather was warm and there was hashish everywhere.

The new city of Tangiers, with its cars and modern buildings, was nice, but nothing like the medina. The buildings were all white and very much like a whiteout if you were trying to get around. It was almost impossible to find places until you had a few days under your belt. Often Blair and I spent the afternoon just drinking a few cups of very hot mint tea at a café beside a small square. We would split any English newspaper we found and often borrowed one from a person sitting near us. This worked far better than buying one, and we met a number of interesting expats this way.

The most fun was to watch a new, unsuspecting tourist arrive into the town square in the middle of the medina. From our great seats in a local café looking out onto the square, we would watch the newcomer be surrounded by the same young kids that went after us on our arrival. They all said they were students, of course, offering to help their victims at no charge. Soon, our newcomer would leave under the direction of two or three of these kids. The students were always trying to find a rich, naive victim, new to the city, so that they could make a great deal of money.

Dinner was always a special occasion and always very late. We and our fellow hitchhikers ate at several restaurants in the medina. The owners were somewhat sympathetic to us and seemed to tolerate our endless bargaining for dinner. The procedure was always the same, and we followed it throughout all of North Africa and the Middle East.

First, we would find a restaurant recommended by other hitchhikers on the same budget as us. Failing that, we would walk until we found a place with hitchhikers in it. Then we would march to the back, to the kitchen, since it was hopeless deciphering the menu in Arabic and far harder to bargain after already sitting down at a table in the restaurant. In this way we communicated that we still had not committed, and our commitment would depend on what deal we could get that night. Most of the dinners were the same: couscous with some sort of meat sauce poured over it, full of spices and vegetables. The owner, usually the cook, would have maybe six different pots of food on the stove. Blair and I would just point to each dish, holding up fingers to indicate the cost and bargain away for a few minutes to get maybe three dishes. After we had agreed on a price, the cook then spooned the food onto a plate. As part of the deal, we would usually offer to eat in the kitchen, at the smallest table, to save nice tables in the restaurant for full-paying customers. Bread was our friend. Baked in small loaves, it was used to scoop up our dinner, a delicious replacement for cutlery.

Besides cost, the advantage of eating in the kitchen was that this was where the action was. The owner's friends would show up, and like us, taste what he was cooking that night, then shout and ramble on in Arabic, with lots of laughing and bargaining back and forth. They would ask us where we were from, then talk to us forever about their politics or how wonderful their city was.

Other hitchhikers were always there, crowded behind the stove. Blair and I would learn what was going on, where to go next and where they had been. By now we had discovered that there was an unspoken yet competitive hitchhikers' code: whoever had been hitchhiking the longest and travelled the farthest obtained the highest status. Usually, anyone who had been to Turkey or farther east won.

After a few hours in the kitchen, it was off to the local hash party, which could last all night. After the novelty wore off, these parties were rather dull affairs. Perhaps six or more of us would sit around a low table on cushions, smoke hashish and listen to Arabic music, which would slowly lull us to sleep. Unlike our times in Nice and southern Spain, there was no wine. Blair and I didn't have a drop from Tangiers onwards until we got to Tunisia.

Most of the locals with a formal education spoke French. I noticed that Blair's French was getting better and better, whereas my French, initially poor, was not improving at all. We spent six days in Tangier and with each passing day became more comfortable. I could see the charm of the city, once we knew what was going on. But for many of the unprepared it was a tale of woe, as they got taken on the day of arrival and lost a lot of money.

Our days of staying only two days in a city were long gone, and even just five days would soon become considered a short visit. When describing those on bus tours, a common saying among our fellow hitchhikers was "If it's Wednesday, it must be Rome, as Tuesday was Paris, and Thursday will be Florence."

It was time to see the rest of Morocco, and our sights were set on Casablanca. Before I left Canada, Casablanca was the only city I had heard of in Morocco, because of the famous movie by the same name. Perhaps we could find Rick's Café Américain. It was only one good day of hitchhiking away. We left the next morning.

After our time in Tangier, Casablanca was disappointing. Because I had seen the movie, my expectations were set by its exotic scenes, but it was far from what was portrayed at Rick's Café. A large city, Casablanca seemed to flow everywhere along the sea. There was a large, boring modern area, and the medina didn't have the same spark as Tangier's.

That afternoon, while we were walking around the medina, an older fellow and his friend from England, who both worked as reporters for the BBC, picked us out. That night there was to be a large party for visiting reporters, and they convinced us that we would be welcome. What attracted us was free booze, a real rarity in Morocco for sure, and just as importantly, a free dinner.

We made our way to the party by local bus and were welcomed warmly. There must have been over fifty well-dressed gentlemen mingling outside in a beautiful low-lit garden with lights strung from tree to tree and a small band playing Arabic music in the corner. However, after a half-hour of raiding the buffet and guzzling a double gin and tonic, both Blair and I noticed a predominance of males in attendance. In fact, it was female free.

We were approached by BBC reporters and others from competing news agencies. We were naive and young, but even we realized by then that this was a strictly gay party and that we had been invited as fresh, new faces for all the expats attending. It was time to get the hell out of there. Not before one last run at the buffet. I grabbed a double Scotch, and off we went.

This was not the first time we were mistaken for being gay. Perhaps it was because we were nineteen and travelling together. The natural assumption, especially among the local Moroccans, was that we were gay and open to approaches. Coming from a small town, this was a rude awakening to how things could be perceived in some parts of the world.

The next afternoon, while Blair and I were hanging out in the medina discussing whether to hitch to Marrakesh and give the rest of Casablanca a miss, we fell in with a parade. It was a wedding celebration, a long procession with a hundred Arabs all yelling and playing drums or flutes. We were told in broken English and French that there was a feast at the end and all were welcome. The feast idea really perked us up, so for over an hour, we walked through the streets, following the parade. Behind all of this were two lambs on a spit, waiting to be devoured. But when we finally got to the house of the bride, we were politely told that this was the end of the road for us. Very disappointing, but still a lot of fun along the way.

For weeks, I had been carrying around a blanket to help with the cold, which somehow got tangled up in my pack in Madrid. It was quite warm in Casablanca even in late November, so I decided to sell it in the market. I got seven dirhams: almost two dollars at the black-market rate. It was time to treat Blair to dinner in Casablanca with my newfound spoils.

We had been told that once one left Tangier, the black market barely existed, due to the police presence. For that reason, we had loaded up on cash prior to leaving Tangier. Since we expected to spend at least ten or more days in Morocco, both Blair and I cashed twenty dollars' worth of travellers' cheques into dirham at the market rate, and thus were flush with cash. I would go on to check my money bag about twenty times a day.

Early the next morning, after just two nights in Casablanca, we were off to Marrakesh to see if all the good things we had been told about that city for the last month were indeed true. Sadly, Casablanca had been a bust and not worth the stopover. Now we hitched south along the sea and then inland, easily making the trip in less than a day.

18

Modern Art with Consequences

As soon as he saw the Big boots, Pooh knew that an adventure was going to happen.

— Winnie the Pooh

For the past month, I had often heard variations of "Wait till you get to Marrakesh, by far the best city in Morocco. You will never want to leave." The second I got there, Marrakesh had me captivated. The primary attraction was the centre of the medina, Jemaa el-Fna Square. Blair and I had never seen anything like it. It was huge, perhaps 750 metres square, crowded with a thousand locals and few tourists. Everything was sold in stalls — orange juice, water in leather bags, fruit, chickens, and meat with flies everywhere. Monkeys were balanced on young kids' shoulders, ready to do their tricks. Snake charmers, with cobras swinging back and forth in front of them, dominated. There were circles of men throughout the square watching magicians or storytellers. At night, the square changed to an outdoor restaurant. Food stalls would move in from nowhere. Often the snake charmers and monkey handlers would still occupy the square in the evening, hoping to find the odd tourist. But tourists were rare to the square after sunset.

Blair and I had been given the name of a small hotel just off Jemaa el-Fna Square. Unlike in Tangier, it didn't feel like every Arab in the city was trying to take us for a ride. We did have the usual problem finding a cheap dive, but rather than rely on kids for directions, we stopped at a few prosperous shops and showed the owner the name of our hotel written in French. Luckily, we found someone who knew exactly where it was, and he took us there directly as a favour.

The hotels we stayed in were not really flophouses. They were clean and cheap, and the owners seemed to work a hundred hours a week, always there to help guests. They were all characters and could get you anything you wanted, for a price. On this occasion it was like we had the benefit of Trip Advisor. It had already been vetted by countless hitchhikers before us, who, over time, had narrowed down the best hotels in Marrakesh for the money. Usually, the recommendations came as a dual package. The mention of a second hotel was for those who had a little more money and appreciated a bit of comfort. The extra cost was really only the equivalent of about a dollar a night, but Blair and I always chose the first option, unless it was a dive.

Since hitchhikers were known to take off in the night, every hotel demanded cash in advance for the room. The payment process often took quite a while, since we never accepted the rate first offered for the night. Sometimes we had to walk out of the hotel when we could not get the right price, which we knew to do from others. For the most part, though, as soon as the owner figured out we already knew what the rooms went for, we came to a quick settlement. If Blair and I were going to stay five days, we would give him three nights' cash in advance, then come back in three days and pay the rest. We would never know if we were going to change our mind, and there was little chance of getting our money back if we did.

While not flophouses, these hotels were a bit down and out, and there was never a bathroom close to our room. It was usually down three flights of stairs in a dark corner somewhere. There would not be a toilet in the bathroom, nor toilet paper. You would have to place your feet on either side of a hole in the ground and use a bucket of water to help clean yourself afterwards.

Hygiene-wise, you had to watch that when you ate; nothing touched your left hand, since that was the hand used when cleaning yourself after going to the bathroom. If a Moroccan saw someone eating with their left hand (I am left-handed), they just couldn't watch. They would consider that person an unclean, barbarian Westerner who didn't have a clue about their country's customs.

By this time, having spent many weeks of perusing international newspapers and seeing famous art in Europe, I considered myself to be quite the intellectual. I took out a number of books from the local library. (I admit to having had no intention of returning them. Today, the books are about fifty-seven years overdue. To relieve my guilt, I would be willing to reimburse that wonderful library in Marrakesh, though I might need a mortgage to pay the fines outstanding.)

My books were by Albert Camus, the French philosopher who wrote about the mid-century uprising in Algeria; *The Heart of Darkness* by Joseph Conrad, which I had read parts of in first-year university and hated; and a large, heavy book of the entire writings of Mark Twain. The idea was to read these books at the side of the road, anticipating long waits for a ride as we crossed North Africa. To fit my new intellectual look, I bought a French beret. To complete the image and give off airs, I added a white Meerschaum pipe, finely carved out of porous, pure white rock. These pipes were the rage at the time, and one could seem very sophisticated talking politics with people from around the world while smoking such a pipe, wearing a beret and perhaps having a book by Camus at one's side.

Each night on the square, we ate in one of the stalls, but kept coming back to the snake charmers, staying just far enough away not to be tackled for some dirham. We waited, hoping a far more affluent American tourist might walk by and be charmed by the cobra. I watched these cobras start to sway back and forth to the music of the charmer, and it was easy to be enticed. Later, we learned from a fellow hitchhiker that the snake charmers were a bit of a scam. The snake had been starved. The only way it could get food was if it heard the noise from the flute of its owner. On hearing the music, the cobra would come straight out of the basked it was trapped in and start weaving back and forth, displaying its fangs. Once the snake got up straight, the owner would give it a morsel of food; this ensured that the next time he played the flute, the snake would again do its schtick. There really wasn't much charming going on — it was just a very hungry snake.

We soon fell into a relaxing way of life in Marrakesh that I have rarely experienced since. We had no timeline. We could stay as long as we wanted and explore the city whenever we wished. There were lots of other hitchhikers in Marrakesh when we got there, some at our hotel but many staying in similar ones all within five minutes or so of the main square. We would meet our friends at small cafés on the square in the early afternoon and order a mint tea.

Mint tea was our replacement for wine. There was no alcohol served, but I assumed that in the expensive hotels in the new French section of town, you could easily get a Scotch or whatever you wanted. The tea was always the same, served very hot. Serving tea was a daily ritual for all Moroccans and a sign of welcome to any guest, including hitchhikers like us. Drinking tea and talking with fellow hitchhikers would take at least an hour or more each day. Because we came back day after day, the waiters tolerated us.

Typically, the waiter would present the tea to us and begin pouring with the pot's spout poised close to one of our tea glasses. As he poured, he would increase the distance and arc of the stream of tea in a continuous motion, then return the pot to the edge of our glass in a grand gesture. You had to drink the tea slowly. In theory, each successive cup of tea out of the same pot tasted different. Blair and I would split a pot between us but were very careful to make sure we each were served three times, even though each serving was only half a cup. Our tea was always served by the same waiter.

"The first glass of tea is bitter as life, the second is as strong as love and the third is as soothing as death," he told us once.

Next to the square were the souks (bazaars) and alleyways. At first, it was like Tangier: very difficult to find one's way around the medina, since the alleys were not straight and wound their way throughout the old city. A stone wall, perhaps thirty feet high, constructed many years ago for defence, encircled the medina. It had a number of famous gates to let people, donkeys and carts in or out, but no cars. If you got lost, at some point you would stumble upon one of these gates and immediately know where you were. The smell of countless herbs and spices was overpowering as we wandered down the alleys, which were full of donkeys, swarms of people pushing carts and the rare motorbike.

Blair and I would just observe. Most of the souk owners spoke a bit of French and after a while would welcome us in French. Days passed quickly, talking to our new friends, seeing other parts of the city and of course, just sitting there watching things while drinking tea.

It took some time to finalize the next steps of our voyage. We would hitchhike back north through the Atlas Mountains to Fez, another must-stop with a large medina not to be missed, then hitch east to the Algerian border. The Morocco–Algeria border was ostensibly open to foreigners only, but we weren't sure. If the border was open, we would need a visa, which could be obtained at the Algerian consulate in Oujda, a large Moroccan city close to the border. When we had arrived in Morocco, we heard there was a lot of tension between the two countries. Just a year earlier, they had fought each other over some disputed area near their respective borders. There were rumours they might close down the border to everyone.

Our plan, now discussed daily over tea, was to hitch all the way across Northern Africa to Cairo, since we had heard that Egypt was even cheaper and just as interesting as Morocco. We would wait out a bit of the winter in Egypt, as it was warm, and hopefully find a way to get to the Middle East, then north to Turkey and finally back to Europe in the early spring. Our plan was rough, but at least it was a route considered by others we met in Marrakesh. Most of our hitchhiker friends, though, were contemplating going back to Spain after Morocco and waiting out the winter with wine, women and song. It was late November, almost December, and Marrakesh was cold. In the early morning, you would freeze if you got up early, as the city was built on a plain high above sea level, right beside the Atlas Mountains. It was not a great place to go to flee the winter.

Blair and I started making lists of places to see and hotels to stay in on our trip across North Africa. Everyone we met was going west to east. We had been unable to find anyone who had done the trip in the opposite direction, from Cairo to Morocco. So we had no first-hand information, only second-hand notes from others who had never been to Algeria. Was it possible to hitchhike, or did one end up walking day after day? We still couldn't find out if we could get across each border. We not only had to cross the Algeria–Morocco border, but those of Tunisia, Libya and Egypt. Lots of tea was consumed over these plans.

Evenings were spent smoking a bit of hash, which we had left over from Tangier, and having our normal dinner of couscous and some sort of meat. The food was good, the people great and the city beautiful. On a clear day, one could see the snow-topped Atlas Mountains rising above the city.

One day, perhaps our sixth in Marrakesh, we noticed a couple of talented artists in the main square drawing a Moroccan scene in chalk on the pavement. Perhaps a hundred locals were crowded around their work, and some were donating to the cause. Every entertainer in the square would do the same thing, and there might be twenty circles of men watching God knows what at any one time. As Blair and I could always do with a few more dirham, this seemed like a great idea, if we could figure out how to entertain the locals. Although neither of us had any artistic ability, perhaps we could try modern art and see what happened. All we needed was some chalk and an open space of pavement in the square to do our act.

I asked the real artists where they had bought their chalk, but they wouldn't tell us, thinking we, too, were artists and would steal their audience. I told them we were no match and were just going to try a few squiggles of modern art and see what happened. They gave in and we found some chalk in the market. Soon we found a small clearing in the square near the ever-present snake charmers. I drew a large circle in chalk, maybe ten metres round, and put my empty beret just inside the circle to collect coins.

Immediately, a number of old men started circling us to see what was going on. They must have been really bored. Blair and I started drawing, at random, a modern art picture of squiggles and fluid lines. We tried to do it with a lot of flourish, flicking our wrists and standing back every minute to admire our handiwork. A new colour was added here, another there, until we were starting to get the outline of a large chalk mess on the pavement.

At this point, I said to Blair, "We're going to have to end this soon. It's looking a little sick, although I must say that my drawings put yours to shame. That mess of yours near the big guy in green, for example. What the hell is that?"

Just then, out of the blue, someone put some money in my beret.

"Look at that," said Blair, with a huge smile on his face. "Jim, that money was obviously meant in appreciation of my work, not yours. I think I'm going to step it up a notch and work on the edges a bit. They need some flair that only I can provide."

Over the next half-hour, the crowd grew to about two hundred men standing in a circle behind our chalk line, watching our production. We just kept adding new colours of chalk in random ways to the pavement, making some sort of modern masterpiece. More and more people were throwing small coins in my beret. We were really getting into it and both started correcting, so to speak, each other's work of art with little squiggles of chalk, then standing up to admire the result. Working the crowd, we received a lot of roars, which we took, of course, as approval of our piece of art.

At first, I missed the distant yet distinctive sound of a siren approaching (a police car in Morocco sounds exactly like a police siren in France: two tones, one higher than the other, annoying but very specific). We noticed a police jeep driving right onto the square, heading directly to our modern-art masterpiece. A driver and his assistant stopped their car only ten metres from

A snake charmer gathering crowds in the same square we would later
improvise in—chalking modern art before a crowd ten times this size.

our work of art and started walking toward us. A scowling gendarme approached and said something in French, which I didn't understand.

"He's telling us that our gig is over and he's demanding that we get into his jeep — now," Blair whispered to me. I grabbed the beret, with maybe fifty small coins in it, and jumped into the back seat of the jeep. We were driven for maybe ten minutes, with two officers in the front seat, and approached an official-looking gate leading to a large colonial building. The driver asked us to follow him and we walked into what was the police station.

The driver took us past many offices, knocked on a large door and ushered us into an enormous office. Some ten metres from the doorway was a police officer with a straight back, no smile, both hands resting on his large desk. In French, he asked us to sit down and said nothing for a long while. Based on his manner and uniform, which had a few stars on it, I figured he must be the guy in charge. This was not looking good.

"Vous êtes très mal comporté dans ma ville," he told us. "Vous essayez de prendre de l'argent a ceux qui sont beaucoup moins fortunés et plus pauvres que vous. Comme jeunes Canadiens, vous devriez, touts les deux, avoir honte de vous-même."

Rough translation: "You have behaved very badly in my city. You are taking money from those far less fortunate than you. As young Canadians, you should both be both ashamed of yourselves."

He looked at Blair, who tried to say a few polite words back in French. When the officer turned to me, I had already decided that my best defence was to declare complete ignorance of the French language, which was not that far from the truth. Besides, why not paint Blair as the bad guy?

"Je ne parle pas de français," I told the official. "I'm sorry."

He then went on again, and I could pick up about every second word. He was telling us, later confirmed by Blair, that it was beneath our dignity to do what we were doing, that we were, in effect, begging, and to accept money from those poorer than us was in exceptionally bad taste. He recognized we had come a long way from Canada, but we needed to understand the culture in Morocco. It was illegal to beg or take money from one not as fortunate. I was thinking, *Thank God we're not in Tangier, or we would be handing over all our money to him to avoid jail.* The thought of even a day in a Moroccan jail was chilling. Thankfully, he was intent on just giving us a lesson in life. But at the end of his speech, he said something in French like, "This is *my* city, and if I ever catch you doing something illegal again, I will not be lenient and will throw the book at you." Right away, we agreed to be little angels. I took the money out of my beret, which I had been clutching during his speech, and put it on his desk. Quickly, we walked out of his office and back to our hotel.

We had been lucky. Very lucky. It could have been far worse. He had made his point, and fifty-seven years later, I still remember his speech. I think it was the right thing to do with two young kids who didn't know better.

After our lecture from the chief of police, Blair and I started thinking. There were lots of rules under the French and Arabic government that we didn't know. What if we inadvertently broke one of their laws while in Marrakesh? Would we be thrown in jail, since it was our second offence? It took Blair and me about two minutes to conclude that perhaps our days of staying in Marrakesh were over. We would either leave that night or early the next morning.

One issue was that we had already paid for two nights at our hotel and only needed one. We needed to get some of that money back. Obviously, if we left the city right away, we would be safer but also poorer. We asked our hotel manager for the next night's rent back. He agreed. As this was rarely done, we thanked him a lot. When we returned to the hotel later that night, we left him a token gift and a note in French saying he was the best hotel manager we had come across on our long voyage.

19

Get Us to the Border

When I got out of school, I spent two years just hitchhiking around. Every time I met some old farmer who could play banjo, I got him to teach me a lick or two. Little by little, I put it together..

— Pete Seeger

We woke up at five in the morning and decided to get out of Dodge that moment. Grabbing our packs, Blair and I started walking in the dark, toward the French Quarter, looking for the highway north up into the Atlas Mountains toward Fez. The medina was poorly lit and vacant, but further on, in the French Quarter, the roads were well lit. We knew the direction of the highway but had no idea where it started. We walked and walked. It was so cold that Blair and I dove into our packs and put on every single piece of clothing we could find. Who would think that as far south as Marrakesh it could get that cold? After going around in circles for a bit, we found the right highway and a good spot to hitch, if only a car would go by. We shivered and waited for any car that was heading north.

A few days earlier, another complication had arrived. Both of us had started getting a mild case of diarrhea. As time went by, it got worse and by the time we had found our hitching spot, it was in full force. Every Westerner seemed to get diarrhea in Morocco. We had been very careful, drinking only bottled water, since the local water was jammed with germs. However, during one of our dinners, I had noticed one of the restaurant employees filling up used water bottles from the tap, putting a seal on them, then putting them back on the shelf to be resold as newly bottled water. I could only conclude that more than one vendor did this. Therefore, at some point, we were going to get the bug.

It had a slightly inappropriate name: the Arab two-step. You walk just two steps, and you go. Another two steps and you go again. What could we do? Since there were only a few people around at five, it was easy just to step off the road for a few minutes and return feeling a bit better, only to repeat. Desperate, I think Blair and I each might have even splurged and paid a dollar for a roll of toilet paper, but sadly, toilet paper wasn't easy to come by in Morocco at this time.

At sunrise, we got our first ride. We felt so relieved to get away from the police and Marrakesh and onto a new adventure. We were headed through the mountains to Fez, probably a two-day hitchhike. But what to do now in the car with the Arab two-step gripping us firmly? After twenty minutes, at most, we explained to our driver, in broken French, that we really needed him to stop at the side of the road. He caught on and pulled over. Blair and I just dove over the side of the road and came back to the car with smiles on our faces.

We worked our way north, with rides of more than twenty minutes presenting a problem, due to our condition. But ultimately, we didn't care and just jumped out of the car to do our thing. After hitching all day in this way, we stopped at a small village and found a hotel, which we hoped would have a room close to the bathroom. It was almost dark when Blair and I started bargaining for the cost of our room. The owner started at an outrageous price. I soon realized that our bargaining position was poor because this seemed to be the only hotel in town.

He had us over a barrel, since it was unlikely we would leave his hotel and start hitching to the next town in the dark. In the end, we paid too much for the room. That night, we thought of a bad idea. It was very cold in the mountains without winter jackets, and the blankets on our bed were wool. We had already told the hotel-keeper that we would be leaving early and not buying breakfast (we could never afford to buy breakfast in the hotels we stayed at). Up very early the next day, Blair and I decided to borrow the two blankets covering our bed and stuff them in our pack. We justified our act over the rate we had to pay for the room; in our view, the blankets certainly evened the game. Today, I still feel bad about this theft, which unfortunately led to a few more instances in the following days.

We used the blankets to keep us warm until a couple of rides came through. In the next town, when the sun was well up and it was getting warm, we found the local market. Nervous as hell, Blair and I each held up a grey blanket with a hotel stripe across the bottom and offered them for sale. My thought was not to get as much as we could for them but to sell them quickly and run. Since you had to ask triple or maybe double what you wanted for something in Morocco, we started at the equivalent of four bucks each.

In an instant, we had buyers offering us the equivalent of a dollar. Since we wanted a fast sale, we gave both blankets to one happy guy for the equivalent of three bucks. At least he was happy, and we now knew that the bottom price for a blanket sold in less than a minute. Three bucks was enough for a deluxe room and dinner for two in a hotel in the next town, or perhaps a room and dinner in Fez, if we were able to get that far.

By this time, I was halfway through reading *The Heart of Darkness*. Conrad's thesis is that we really don't know what we will do when put into certain circumstances. He takes it to the extreme: you might find yourself murdering someone in one case, whereas in regular life, you would never even contemplate killing a fly. It was the same for us. In my sheltered life in Canada, the thought of stealing blankets would be so wrong. I would never be able to even consider such a thing. But here, far away, with little money and struggling to survive, I had warped my thoughts into believing it might be okay to steal blankets, if we needed the money. The chance of getting caught was worth the gain.

This was not the last time we tried this. The hitchhiking was poor in these mountains in the middle of nowhere, and we wouldn't reach Fez until the next day. It was on to yet another small hotel in an unknown town to repeat the same thing.

The next morning we reached Fez and stumbled upon John, one of the hitchhikers we had met in Tangier, just outside the gates to the medina. We greeted each other, and then I had an idea.

"John, we have a couple of blankets that seemed to have found their way into our packs. This looks like a good place to get rid of them. Just wondering if you could hold up one of the blankets with me, and then Blair can get a great picture of us both. We will try to sell them really quick — like less than two minutes — and cut you in on our proceeds."

John, being a bit stupid like us, helped us out, and those blankets were sold in less than a minute for a real bargain.

Fez is really a big city with an enormous medina, far larger even than the one in Marrakesh. This medina was truly a maze

John and I selling hotel blankets at the main entrance to the Medina in Fez.
They were sold in less than two minutes. Note the beret.

of very narrow streets barely wide enough for a donkey, with no straight line in sight. It seemingly trapped you; once you were in, you could never get out. Our only choice was to walk around in random circles, hoping to recognize a shop that might give us a clue as to where we were. The city was less international than Marrakesh. Mick Jagger was not lurking in a café on the square. There were fewer tourists, no monkeys to be seen and no starved snakes rising out of straw baskets. The city was set on seven hills, with the medina in the valley in between.

Just like in other Moroccan cities, in order to find the hotel "just inside the medina" that everyone had recommended, we had to overcome a lot of bad advice from the group of small kids who surrounded us. After a long hike, we discovered the hotel on a side street in the middle of the medina. John, still tagging along, said he was staying at least a kilometre away but would join us for dinner that night (which was on us for his help selling the blankets) and would meet us at our hotel later, where together we could seek a suitable (i.e., cheap) restaurant.

Perhaps Marrakesh had worn us out. After just one night, our thoughts were to try one more night and just get going to Oujda and the Algerian border. The draw to hitch across North Africa as soon as possible was too strong to stay in Fez even a day longer. Perhaps we were goal-oriented, but once we had made the decision to cross into Algeria, we wanted to get there as soon as possible. Our route was to hitch east to Oujda, get our visa, then find a way through the mountains to the nearby Algerian border.

Leaving Fez, the hitching was slow, and once again Blair and I ended up in a small town in the evening, getting yet another room in a crappy but clean hotel. One good thing was that by now the Arab two-step was fading and our bodies were finally used to anything we put into our mouths.

The next morning, Blair and I once again tried the borrow-the-blankets routine. Hitching to the next small town, we held out our blankets for sale, but there were no takers, regardless of price. At this point, it was crazy to push our luck, so we found an older guy huddled up against the curb and gave him our two blankets to keep him warm. That was the end of the blanket game for us. We were starting to feel a bit guilty, and besides, the risk of jail and a fine was not worth the money.

The next day, we plowed on to the city of Oujda, which was an interesting stop. Our task was to find the Algerian consulate and obtain a visa to allow us to enter Algeria. We were not prepared for the paperwork required. First, we needed two passport-type photos before they would even look at us. Finding a photographer and arranging for those pictures took the rest of the day. The next day, we showed up at the Algerian consulate just as they opened, only to be told that Blair's picture, which was not perfectly centred, was not acceptable and needed to be redone.

Returning with a fresh photo of Blair (I think it was really his face that made the picture unacceptable), we filled out countless forms in duplicate and attached our photos to the forms. We took our passports, plus the equivalent of three dollars each, and shoved our passports and the package of forms through the wicket to the ever-so-serious clerk. The problem was that few applied for a visa to Algeria, and these clerks needed to keep their job. It took hours to process something that should have been done in five minutes. With just one complaint from us, our visas would be lost in the bureaucracy, to surface days later. The good news was it appeared the border was open to foreigners — unless the Algerian government was running a scam.

There was another problem: we had too much money. Due to our blanket caper, we had not spent all our dirhams. When we had arrived in Oujda, we had the equivalent, between the two of us, of almost five dollars' worth of dirhams in our pockets. We had thought we would simply exchange our dirhams for local currency once in Algeria, but soon found out that was going to be impossible. Algeria did not recognize Morocco's currency. Dirhams were useless in Algeria.

Blair and I solved most of this problem by considerably upgrading our hotel in Oujda. We got rid of the rest by having a feast in one of the better restaurants in town. When we woke up the next day, we had eighteen cents to make it to Algeria.

With our new visa in hand, we set out for the border but unfortunately could not find a road that led there. It didn't seem to exist. After asking everyone, we found an empty road leading nowhere. It was supposed to lead to the Algerian border, but with no signs and no vehicles, there was no assurance we were on the right road. This wasn't a case of no one picking us up; it was as if someone had taken all the cars away and the border had just been closed. The locals told us it was open to foreigners but hard to cross, and we were on the right road. With no alternative, we just walked the rest of the day into the hills with our heavy packs. Eventually, we reached a tired-looking border crossing.

No one was there except a few large transport trucks. It seems that trucks were allowed to cross the border, and this was a good sign, since perhaps we could grab one from the border into Algeria. The bad news was that the Algerian border hut was still another five kilometres away. This was just a checkpoint on the Moroccan side. Blair and I walked the five kilometres and presented our passports and visas, which disappeared into the depths of the border guard's office behind the one wicket staffed by Mr. Mean. We waited and waited.

This was a game played by the border officials. After a half hour of waiting, travellers with money would demand their passports back. The border-guard guys would talk of their process but in the end would accept a bribe, and voila, here is your passport and you are on your way.

There was no chance we would pay a bribe, so we would just have to wait them out. Having taken almost a day to get here, it looked like a fine place to camp for the night. Finally, after a two-hour waiting game, we got our passports back due only to a shift change. I assumed they had given up on us as a source of funds.

Our new border guards were far nicer. During all this waiting time, only a couple of trucks had arrived at the border. It was not exactly a booming business. Since it was now dark, our new friends the border guards asked if we wanted to stay the night and sleep in a very small cabin-like structure right across from the border. In the morning, things would be better. Maybe we could get a ride with one of the trucks that were sure to cross in the morning. We leapt at the chance. The border guards brought us hot tea and a couple of bowls of who knows what to eat. They were exceptionally kind and quite a contrast to the guys on duty earlier. Later, we found out that this kind of hospitality was the new normal from the citizens of Algeria.

We were not prepared for Algeria. Less than three years earlier, in 1961, Algeria fought and won its independence from the French. Now newly independent, they were ecstatic to show travellers from the outside world what a great country they lived in. The new border guards were the start of the most enthusiastic people, intent on ensuring that we came away thinking Algeria was one of the greatest countries in the world.

We were up with the chickens the next day, given a few cups of hot tea by the border guards, and off we went. Rather than wait for a truck, Blair and I walked down the hills to where we were told there was a small Algerian village. Finding a few parked cars in the village showed us that cars did exist in this area of the world after all.

Our hopes for a ride improved considerably.

20

Jails and More Border Hassles

Money is better than poverty, if only for financial reasons.

— Woody Allen

The very first car leaving the village picked us up. Immediately, our driver asked in French, "Are you hungry?" Blair and I nodded.

"I'll find you somewhere to eat at an outdoor stand along the side of the highway," he said as he drove us east, the right direction. After sharing a great meal of shish kebabs prepared by a local guy in a shack along the road, we were dropped off in the middle of nowhere. Full and happy, we got another ride within a few minutes.

"Algeria is beautiful, beautiful country," our new driver told us. "The people are all like me, best in the world, very wonderful people. Wonderful. You will see. Very friendly. So proud."

He thumped his chest with one hand, keeping the other on the steering wheel. After less than half an hour, he told us, "I treat you lunch." Blair and I would never turn down a free lunch, even if it came thirty minutes after just eating. Off we went to lunch, again.

We were making slow progress due to all the food stops, but we were full. This treating us to lunch, breakfast or dinner went on and on throughout all of Algeria. We were constantly entertained and fed. On our second day, one guy insisted we stay in his home. We met his family, parents and kids, and were given a small room to ourselves. Again, before leaving, we were treated to another breakfast, lots of tea and genuine, warm goodbyes.

Blair and I could not believe the generosity of the Algerians. The hitching was amazing. We would get rides after waiting maybe ten minutes, compared to many hours in Spain or France. And we were spending no money.

We had heard from a fellow in Fez that we could go to a local jail in the evening and ask if they would put us up for the night, then just walk out free the next morning. On our third night, Blair and I passed through the large city of Algiers. Since the hitching was so good, we were able to go right through the city without walking more than a kilometre. We walked through to the eastern suburbs, and there we found a police station in a rather sorry-looking building. We thought it must contain a few jail cells. Hopefully, one of them would be empty.

Blair, the French master, went into the station first and asked if there was any way we could sleep in their jail for the night. In broken French, he explained that we were a bit down on cash while hitchhiking across northern Africa, and that their hospitality would be greatly appreciated. We were lucky. The officers broke into great smiles and laughter and said they would be pleased to have some Canadian guests that night. Blair and I didn't press our luck to ask for dinner. We found a food stand, bargained for our dinner, then went back to the police station to be given one of their best rooms. It did have bars, but we each had a twin to ourself and were given a lot of tea. Soon, other police were coming by, wanting to practise their English with us. It looked like we would never get to sleep. This seemed like a very good way to save money, meet more Algerians and have a good night's sleep. As we crossed North Africa, we would now try to find a small town at night with a police station and, hopefully, spend the night safe and sound.

The next morning, the officers gave us a huge breakfast with lots of hugs and kisses and even more tea. The irony of our situation was not lost on us: we had given up stealing blankets in fear of getting caught and thrown in jail, and yet now we cozied up to our potential captors in their own prison, leaving free in the morning.

Walking back to the highway from the jail, I noticed far more women than usual on the streets. All were covered in dark-coloured clothing, and if lucky you could see their eyes peeking through a veil. I assumed the women were shopping for food and just came out of their homes in the morning and spent the rest of their day cooking, cleaning and perhaps working in the garden. The status of women in North Africa appeared to us to be far lower than in Europe and North America. For example, we realized that not once had a woman been in a car that had picked us up since we left Gibraltar. Women never drove and were rarely passengers in cars.

In the larger cities it was the same, though we did see women in the markets shopping for food. All the shopkeepers were men. Not a woman in sight. I can't even recall talking to a local woman as we crossed North Africa. Seen rarely and not heard. We understood that Arab women were in charge at home and controlled the household. But on the streets, they were rarely seen and kept to the background.

Most of our rides were with large transport trucks. In some of them, both of us could squeeze into the front cab and throw our packs in the back. Each driver was always the owner of the truck, and every truck was colourfully decorated to suit his personality. Pictures of his family were everywhere; orange and green tassels might be hanging from the sun visor, and a row of bright red fringe covered the armrest. *Colourful* was the name of the game. Eccentric, by our taste, but certainly not boring. Every trucker smoked, with one hand on his precious cigarette and the other gesturing to make a point as he spoke to Blair and me in French. Sometimes we wondered who was actually driving the truck. It looked like these trucks just drove by themselves.

On one of our longest rides in Algeria, there was no way both Blair and I would fit in the front cab. One of us had to sit outside in the back of the truck, in the open with our packs, and the other would get the front seat. We flipped a coin. I lost. At this point Blair was revelling in his French skills, going on and on to each driver in French and laughing at his own jokes, while I sat silent. At least while stuck in the back, I would not have to listen to Blair.

This particularly long hitch was not a comfortable ride. All the drivers drove as fast as they could, but this guy drove as if he was trying to win the Monaco Grand Prix. For over three hours, I rode with my back against the cab, jostled up and down on a sack of vegetables as he drove faster and faster. As he wheeled around corners, I hung on to anything I could. Through the cab window, I could see Blair moving his hands back and forth, having a great time talking to our driver. When we finally stopped at the driver's destination, he came over to me and gave me a giant hug. He wouldn't let go. The driver was almost crying, and he told me in French that things would work out, to keep going, and that God and Allah would be my salvation.

I wondered what had prompted such an emotional reaction. As the driver drove off, I asked Blair, "Okay, what the hell is going on?"

"The trip in the cab was boring, so I decided to tell the driver that you were an orphan who had lost his parents early in life and been cast aside. My parents had taken pity on you and had managed to free you from the orphanage."

I couldn't believe this.

Blair continued. "I told him that after a year or so in our home, you had become very sick and, unfortunately, it was a terminal illness. I had agreed to show you the world before you passed on. Now, here we were in the great country of Algeria."

You just had to laugh — I was still not happy about having lost the toss for the front seat, but I was somewhat amazed at Blair's ingenuity in this story.

We were making very good time charging across northern Algeria, heading toward Tunisia, the next country along the north coast of Africa. It had only taken five days after entering Algeria, and we were approaching the area where the traffic disappeared near the border. Since locals rarely, if ever, crossed their border into another country, the only traffic coming and going across all the borders in North Africa were large transport trucks.

Not a single car was on the road. Like the border into Algeria, it looked like we had no alternative except to walk to the border. In Morocco, we had been told that you did not need a visa to enter Tunisia from Algeria if you were Canadian, so why spend bucks on a visa if it was not needed?

However, we were not counting on what had happened a few days earlier. Apparently, two Canadians had robbed a local store near the border and roughed up the owner. They had been caught at the border trying to get into Tunisia and were thrown in jail. To say the least, the mood toward Canadians at this particular moment was not good. Unfortunately, we happened to be the next Canadians to attempt to cross the border into Tunisia.

The border police claimed we needed a visa. We knew it was not true.

Americans did require a visa, but several Australians had told us the British Commonwealth countries were exempt. Blair and I asked where we could get such a visa, perhaps here at the border (meaning take our two bucks and send us on), but they gave us two alternatives: we could go back to Algiers, the capital of Algeria, to the main consulate for Tunis, which was at least two or three days of hitching, or go to Constantine, a large city we had passed on the way some five hundred kilometres west of us. There, a small consulate was open on and off and could perhaps give us a visa.

We had no alternative if we wanted to continue to Cairo. So, we turned around and started walking down the hills back into Algeria, heading for Constantine. Few cars crossed the border and none were going away from the border heading west. Despite how wonderful the citizens were, we felt bitter. A five-hundred-kilometre detour and the cost of another visa had not been in our cards.

We were lucky, though. The first car that came through the border picked us up. From this point on, it was easy pickings as we headed due west. Our next ride was in a Mercedes with two guys in suits heading for a town less than a hundred kilometres from Constantine. A ride of almost 350 kilometres in a Mercedes was a dream. I should mention that our hitchhiking style in North Africa had changed a lot from what we did in, say, Germany. Blair and I no longer hitched meekly on the side of the road only to curse as a driver went past us in a cloud of dust. After a while, we had learned that you get about a quarter of the way onto the highway so the driver is forced to swerve a bit to get around you. If you lose this car, it might be another half hour or more before you see another one. It was sort of a game of chicken, because we really didn't want to get run over, but the Algerian people were so kind, they realized we needed a ride and stopped all the time.

Halfway through our ride, the driver told us we were stopping for lunch and they were going to take us to a famous restaurant that specialized in baked sheep's head. What could we say? We were not going to give up on our ride, which still had two hours to go, to avoid having to eat a sheep's head. Our plan was to get to Constantine that night and start the visa application process early the next morning. We were hoping no additional pictures were required, and it would just be a big stamp on our already crowded passport and few signatures to please the border guards.

As we walked into the restaurant, I saw on a number of tables half a sheep's head sitting on a plate, steaming away, to be devoured by happy Algerians. In the kitchen were a number of small ovens; in each one was a sheep's head, baked for God knows how long. In rapid Arabic, our hosts ordered for us. After a short wait, when the sheep's head was fully cooked and steaming, a waiter came out of the kitchen with a very heavy knife and, in front of the table, cut the damn thing right in half. We each had half a sheep's head sitting on a plate in front of us. It was not that appealing.

The first thing I noticed was the eyeball that stared right at me. I was hoping it was only decoration, but no, this was part of the feast. The head came with lots of warm flat bread and various dipping sauces. We were to eat it with our hand, making sure the left hand never touched a thing. Our driver demonstrated the proper way to eat sheep's head. First, he scraped a bit of meat off the head with his knife, covered it in sauce, then stuffed the meat inside a rolled-up piece of flatbread. He didn't pick at it like we were doing but instead gulped down the entire piece in one go with great relish.

We managed a few bites and discovered it was not that bad at all, but then Blair and I had to face the dreaded eyeball, which just sat there, daring us to eat it.

Again, the driver gave us a demonstration. He scooped the eyeball out of the sheep's head with a spoon, placed it between the bread, added the required sauce, and ate it down in one gulp. We knew this was our moment of truth: either eat the eyeball and continue our ride, or walk away and find another ride. We closed our eyes and both ate an eyeball at the same moment, knowing our hosts would be ecstatic.

Throughout the whole meal, these guys were laughing, watching our reactions. We had lots of toasts of hot tea to our success. They hit us on the shoulder, smiled and laughed, as they were now showing Westerners a real feast. I have no idea what this lunch cost, but it was far above our budget. We were relieved when the driver and his companion went to the cashier and paid for the entire meal.

Two hours later, Blair and I were hitchhiking on the side of the road, only an hour from our destination on a good highway. We could easily be in Constantine before nightfall. We intended to find a hotel and be first in line at the Tunisian consulate office the next morning. Hopefully, it would be open and we could get the visa and get the hell out of there.

To our surprise, Constantine was a visually dramatic city. Having breezed right through it on the way to the Tunisian border, we now saw that it was built around a massive gorge with eight narrow steel bridges crossing everywhere we looked.

One of the bridges, built in 1912, was said to be the highest one in the world until 1929, at a height of 175 metres. The gorge must have been two hundred metres wide and one hundred metres deep, and it split the city in half. From everywhere in the city, I could see at least one of these bridges and peer down to the depths of the gorge. We almost decided to spend another night in the city and explore the gorge and the medina, but it was time to keep moving. Besides, with my fear of heights, there was no way that I would have lasted even ten seconds on top of one of those bridges. Blair would have had to peel me off the cables holding up the bridge and take me home, blubbering.

We were on the front steps of the consulate the second it opened. To make sure the officials were on our side, we made up a story that the purpose of our trip to Tunisia was to see the ancient city of Carthage, built many centuries ago. We told them we had heard Tunisia was such a beautiful country with such warm people, etc. It didn't hurt to lay it on, as having a consulate clerk who liked us could cut down our wait time considerably. After probably an hour, and paying the equivalent of about two bucks, less than we had thought and coincidentally what we had considered offering as a bribe, they stamped a full page of our passport with their visa, signed it and said we could now enter their country. We didn't even ask whether we really needed this visa. We paid and got out of there. *Happy* wasn't the word.

It was time to hitch back up to the border crossing where we had been just thirty-six hours ago. Although the hitching was as good as before, we needed quite a few rides. As usual, the closer we got to the border, the fewer cars there were. It became obvious we were going to have to stay another night in Algeria before making the border. We spent it in a miserable little town in the hills close to the main road that went across North Africa.

The visa at last, issued to us by the Consul General of Tunis on December 17, 1964, which allowed us to finally enter Tunisia.

This had to be the dirtiest town we had stayed in. Dust was everywhere. Checking into the crumbling old structure that was pretending to be a hotel, we couldn't get the dirt off our packs or clothes.

The mattresses seemed to touch the floor before we even crawled into the beds. A night in jail would be far preferable to this place.

Early the next day, Blair and I walked through the various border crossings, finally getting to the last one, which had turned us away. The Tunisian border guards were not the same ones who had sent us back three days ago. We handed over our passports, complete with visas, with not a word from the guards. What the border guards were really looking for was a stamp showing we had been to Israel. Finding an Israeli stamp could have resulted in us being thrown in the local jail and certainly denied access to their country.

In their eyes, anyone who had been to Israel or planned to go was a traitor and should be punished. We never even mentioned the word *Israel*. It was spoken in hushed terms because to be heard mentioning the word might cause someone to report us to the authorities. To some guards, the review of our passports was a power trip. We had to stay calm because they held all the cards and we didn't have the money to pay them to get ourselves out of a jam.

The guards always noticed the Checkpoint Charlie and Smoky Joe's stamps in our passports and waved their fingers, telling us these were not countries and we should never have such stamps, which made the passport illegal. As most hitchhikers had done the same, the best defence was to say nothing. It was just another ploy to get a few extra dollars from us. What Blair and I wished for was to have the guard notice and focus on someone with a bit of money directly behind us in the lineup. The guards were not stupid. They realized there was a lot more money in it for them from a couple of well-dressed Americans behind us than from two wretched young Canadians. Finally, after a two-hour wait, out popped our passports. The guards had given up trying to extract anything from Blair and me and just wanted to be rid of us.

21

A Night in Tunisia

Tourists don't know where they've been, travelers don't know where they are going.

— *Paul Theroux*

At last, we were in Tunisia. Like Morocco and Algeria, it had been a French colony until recently; it had achieved its independence in 1962. But Tunisians were not as proud as Algerians to show off their independence. At first, they didn't seem very friendly at all, which was quite a contrast with Algeria.

Like at all border crossings, Blair and I started walking, since the chance of a car coming was slim. Local traffic would start about ten kilometres from the border, and that was a long way to walk. The weather was fair, Blair's company was great and we were over halfway to Cairo from Tangiers. After an hour's walk, we came across an orange grove along the side of the road. Since we were starved, Blair decided to jump the fence and pick a few. Just as he was coming back to the road with six or so large oranges, the owner caught him. Blair explained, in French, that we had just come from Algeria to his wonderful country and were starved. After listening, he went back to his orange grove

Blair hungry and foraging for oranges just off the road somewhere in Tunisia.

and gave us more oranges. Not only that, he drove us down the road to the nearest town in his ancient open truck. We sat in the back of his truck, eating his oranges, feeling very happy with life. It was a good start.

I had told the clerk at the Tunisian consulate we wanted to visit the ruins of Carthage, and we found that they were just a short distance from the Tunisian capital, Tunis. So as we approached Tunis, we left the main highway and hitched north to Carthage. It was getting late, and our last ride took us to a reasonably sized town close to Carthage.

It was jail time again. We found one of the better jails so far, and it had some empty cells. The Tunisian police, like Algerians, allowed us to sleep the night in an empty cell as long as there was not a crime spree. In that moment I considered writing a Michelin-style guide book rating each of the North African jails we had stayed in for comfort, accessibility while hitchhiking, food, service and extras, but never quite got around to it. This jail was a solid five stars. The police seemed to like the change of pace with our stay, and like always, we had about ten cups of tea, listening to them tell their stories in French. Of course, I pretended to understand and Blair tried to show off, laughing at the right moments.

The next day, hitching to Carthage was easy. Blair and I were surprised to see tourists at the site, since we had not seen a single one since leaving Marrakesh. None were hitching, of course. A large bus stood parked by the ruins, which hinted that they were all on the same tour. For the first time in a month, we could speak English to others. We scared these English tourists with stories of our travels, including the eyeball meal. We slipped into their tour to find out from their guide what had happened at this site, because all we were seeing was a lot of fallen stones from buildings that must have been constructed thousands of years ago.

Carthage had been a real powerhouse that even rivalled Rome. We could see the old port, which we were told was one of the busiest in the entire Mediterranean 2,500 years ago. Unfortunately for the citizens, Rome conquered them, and at the height of the Roman empire, the city was transformed into a mini-Rome. An ancient outdoor theatre had been built, plus extensive Roman baths and villas. Blair and I were impressed and spent most of the day there, before hitching south a short way to the large city of Tunis.

Like in France, where all roads led to Paris, all roads in Tunisia led to Tunis. Therefore, it was a quick hitch. Luckily, or perhaps unluckily, we were dropped off in the very centre of the city. Tunis was a surprise. It was a modern city, with high-rise office towers, new, modern hotels, and cafés lining the streets full of people drinking beer and wine. This was unlike anything else we had seen so far in North Africa, where alcohol was banned. In such a large city, staying in the local police station did not seem like a great idea. Blair and I doubted that a large police station would even give us the time of day. So we headed for the old town on foot, where we could find a hostel for the night and grab dinner. The next day, we could obtain our visas for both neighbouring Libya and Egypt, which we expected would take all day.

We were very focused on getting to Cairo to meet our fellow hitchhikers, who planned to be there around Christmas. We had also met a fellow hitchhiker in Tangier named David, a very outgoing guy, always dressed in army fatigues, and he was going to hitch solo across North Africa to Cairo. He told us that we needed to get together for a New Year's party in Cairo, since he was meeting a few of his buddies there. Although we still had over two weeks to reach Cairo, our minds were not on seeing all the sights of Tunis but to keep moving.

By chance, we started talking to a well-dressed middle-aged local in a suit. He was in town on business, lived in another city and told us he would love some company. He offered to buy us dinner at one of the nearby cafés. So off we went, and not only had a great meal but a beer as well, all on our new friend. He was quite a bit older than us but seemed very interested in our travels and impressions of Tunisia. He talked of Libya, where we were going next, and told us that you went to Libya to work and earn money, but you went to Tunis to play.

After dinner, our new companion mentioned that he had not yet found a hotel to stay the night, but we were welcome to share the room with him if we wanted. He said that he was going to pay for a room anyway, and an extra bed would not cost a cent more. True to his word, we went into a large, luxury-skyscraper-type hotel, right in the middle of the city, that catered to business travellers. Blair and I could not believe how lucky we were to have bumped into this guy. We would have the luxury of running water and a real bathroom.

It was late, so when we got to his room, we all took turns using the bathroom. The room had one very large bed and one single. Right away, our new buddy jumped into the large bed. Blair and I decided to both squeeze into the single.

After a few minutes, our new friend asked, in French, "Who's first?" He opened the covers on his side to make room for one of us to jump into bed with him.

My brain started working. There were two of us and he was not a big guy, but what if he had a knife or gun? Blair and I stared at each other, then at him.

"We'll just stay where we are," Blair told him in French. Still waiting for one of us to join him, the man kept looking at me. Perhaps he preferred me over Blair?

We stayed put.

In broken French, Blair started yelling back at the man. I yelled to Blair, "Tell him we will call the manager of the hotel." Only one problem: the phone was right beside the man's bed and we were at least a good five metres away. My other idea was to make a run for the door. One of us could get down to the lobby and raise a fuss. But that would leave one of us alone with this guy, which was not a good idea. We could both run, but we had laid out all of the stuff from our packs on the floor and couldn't afford to lose all our possessions. (Our pouches with our passports and money were with us in bed, since they never left us.)

Finally, Blair came up with a good idea. He told the guy, "We're calling the police. One of us is going down to the lobby to bring the police back to this room." The mention of police seemed to have a lot more effect than calling the manager.

Although he started screaming at us, we could see he was getting dressed. In a minute or two, he was gone.

I can't believe my radar did not start going off at the mention of the hotel room. Perhaps the word *free* had made my brain go into hibernation. The fact that he had no luggage might have been our first clue. How could two people who had been travelling for about five months be so naive?

At first, Blair and I could not believe he was gone. We put the chain on the door.

"How the hell did we ever agree to share his room?" asked Blair, who looked exceptionally relieved that our host was gone.

"It was the lure of the free room," I replied. "He sounded great. You remember when we first met him. He bought us dinner. Seemed like a real nice guy."

"Let's face it. We were lucky. What if he had had a knife or wouldn't leave? What the hell were we going to do then?" Blair continued, "I think he was really interested in you."

I wasn't sure if Blair, thinking of himself as the more attractive of the two of us, was disappointed or relieved at this observation.

We both looked at the shower at the same time. One of the things you miss most when hitching and staying in jails or cheap hotels is a shower. Blair and I would stay in hostels at least once a week, if we could find them, just for the opportunity to get a shower. Most hostels had coin-operated showers. You would put in, say, the equivalent of five cents and lather your hair with soap, then the damn hot water would cut off and you would need to jam in another coin. It often took three or four coins to do the trick.

This time, no coins. We each had a long, half-hour shower, so long that the water started running out of the bathroom onto the carpet. Soon, there was a small lake. I looked around the room for any goodies that might be for sale, and sure enough, four or five Swiss chocolate bars found their way into our packs, as well as a number of other treats.

Blair deciphered the checkout instructions and found that we needed to be gone at noon. We flipped for the large bed, and I won. Things were really looking up. We slept until ten, had yet another shower and expanded the size of the lake in the room. We were able to use real toilets, brushed our teeth ten times and felt like a million bucks.

We were worried the guy might have said something to the hotel desk as he left the night before, and we didn't want them to check up on the condition of the room, the missing treats, or far worse, charge us for the room. With our wits back in fine form, Blair and I got off the elevator on the third floor, found the stairs, walked down, out of sight of the front desk, and ran — with smiles on our faces.

22

The Argument

I have found out there ain't no surer way to find out whether you like people or hate them than to travel with them.

— Mark Twain, Tom Sawyer Abroad

Blair and I were still in happy mode following our never-ending hot showers. It was noon, and the objective for the day was to get our visas in Tunis for nearby Libya and Egypt. (We had been told it was far easier to get an Egyptian visa at their embassy in Tunis than to wait till we got to Libya.) When the Egyptian embassy told us that it would take at least twenty-four hours to process our visa, it really didn't upset us as it normally would have. However, when we found out we had to surrender our passports to the embassy for twenty-four hours, meaning we would need to wait yet another twenty-four hours to submit them to the Libyan embassy while they went through the same routine, our mood crashed.

A change in plan was in order, since we would have to spend at least two more nights, probably three, in Tunis while we waited for our documents to be returned. We needed to obtain the required pictures, taken in the correct size and form, and submit everything to the Egyptian embassy that afternoon before they closed. Without our passports, there was no sense ambling over to the Libyan embassy to apply for their visa, but we did drop by just to confirm the ground rules, including the type of picture required. They confirmed it would take at least twenty-four hours to process our visas.

After all of this, we were not in the mood to stay the night in another jail. Luckily, in my notes I had the name of a recommended hotel in Tunis, which was, of course, in the middle of the medina. When we got to the hotel, close to dinner time, we found that once again we knew a few of their guests from earlier times.

One fellow we had spent a lot of time with in Morocco went by the name of Bill — no last name. We had last seen Bill in Oujda, heading for the Algerian border. Bill was about thirty-three, far older than us, had a large bushy beard and was from California. Outgoing and super friendly, he had been on the road for ten years. Yes, ten years, and he had arrived in Tunis two days earlier, was staying in our hotel and loved the city. We also met four characters from Berlin, travelling in a very crowded Volkswagen bus, who were taking a few nights off from sleeping in their cramped van.

These guys had an off-and-on relationship with a woman we called Dizzy, who, on occasion, slept in their van and was bold enough, or stupid enough, to be hitching alone across North Africa. Being a blonde woman hitchhiking solo in North Africa was not a good combination. For some reason, Arab men thought that if any woman, particularly a blonde, was doing this, she was very open and looking for sex. Since this was almost an insurmountable problem, most if not all women we met had joined up with men in the very challenging hitchhike across North Africa.

We had met Dizzy earlier in Morocco and spent an evening having dinner with her and her then beau. Dizzy was a good-looking, five-foot-nothing, outgoing blonde. She was always jumping around and seemed a bit light-headed. Perhaps that's why everyone called her Dizzy. We were unsure if she had a current romantic relationship with one of our German friends, or all of them, but they were protecting her.

That night, Blair and I went for dinner with Bill at a hitch-hiker's restaurant, eating in the kitchen as usual. He assured us that Tunis was a wonderful city and well worth seeing. Now that we had bumped into Bill, Blair and I were much happier, even though we were stuck in Tunis for a few days. In minute detail, we told him about our escapades of the previous night in a four-star hotel.

For the next two days, we explored the medina, with Bill entertaining us with stories of his ten years of travel. Most of the medina was covered in vines. Tiny beams of light came through to the shops below. I found more than ten shoe stores in a row, which put Madrid to shame. When not wandering the medina, we spent a lot of those two days in the American library. The American libraries always had copies of the major English-language newspapers. Perhaps they were out of date by as much as a week, but to someone with no knowledge at all of what was happening in the world, one week was nothing.

That night, a highlight was when Bill took us to a 'den', really a hole in the wall full of smoke, where Blair and I could experience smoking a water pipe known as a hookah. The hookah didn't come with a book of instructions, so it took us almost half an hour to get it going. We were cheap, so the idea was to share one of these contraptions among the three of us. In the hookah you smoke a tobacco mixture, known as shisha, that comes in several flavours. The water is heated by charcoal.

We chose a flavour and paid our money, much to the laughter of the locals.

It really was not that appealing, but we could tell the locals were amused and perhaps impressed with us attempting the hookah. We didn't want to disappoint. Despite countless attempts at using this contraption with little success, we were determined to make the best of it. I guess success was finally drawing some of the foul-tasting smoke into our lungs and avoiding a coughing fit. From that day onwards, I was never tempted again to try this smoke-eating machine.

The good news was that our visas were ready on time. Blair and I had spent the equivalent of $17.50 on visas and pictures to cross North Africa, roughly the same amount we had spent on hotels and meals. The bad news was that we got our second visa very late in the day, too late to start our hitch to the Libyan border that night. Bill, on the other hand, already had his visas. Since trying to get a ride while hitching with three across the desert was almost impossible, he had headed out early that morning with an agreement that we would meet him in Egypt.

We would leave early in the morning in the hope of making the four hundred kilometres to the Libyan border in one day. This was a pipe dream, since there was almost no chance we could go that far once we got near the border. The number of cars and trucks on the road was sure to drop to near zero. On the way, we wanted to stop over and see the coliseum in El Djem, about two hundred kilometres east of Tunis. Apparently, the structure rivalled the coliseum in Rome and was a must-visit. It was right on the highway to the official border crossing.

For some reason, the hitching the next day was good, and well before noon, there was the amphitheatre sitting out in the middle of nowhere. It was massive and must have sat fifty thousand spectators in its time. It had been built at the height of the Roman empire for gladiator shows, fighting lions and chariot races. I was in awe. Here it was in magnificent shape, looking much like the day it was constructed. Sitting on one of the thousands of stone seats, you could almost see a chariot race in front of you.

Why was it built here, though, in the wide-open desert, so far from a major city? In the early third century, the Romans had built a large city on this spot that rivalled Carthage as the second most important city in North Africa. Today, there was only a village left, dominated by its amphitheatre. The city was gone. Being in the middle of nowhere meant there were very few tourists exploring the theatre. It was eerie seeing this gigantic theatre so well preserved in the middle of the desert with few, if any, buildings surrounding it.

We had woken up in very bad moods and were on each other for the entire trip to El Djem. I would open my mouth, and Blair would be all over me for something. It seemed anything we did that morning was upsetting. We had been together every day since Gibraltar, almost a month ago. There was no escaping each other for meals, sleeping and hitchhiking. It was face to face whether you liked it or not.

We started arguing about how the other was hitchhiking. Blair was not putting enough effort into the job. I was not appreciating that he had to do all the talking in French, as I was too stupid to learn the language. Since everything we did that day seemed to get on the other's nerves, we stopped talking to each other early that morning.

After a relatively short tour of the ruins, Blair and I were on the road again and soon had a ride of only forty kilometres, after which we waited and waited. It wasn't that the cars were not stopping for us, it was that there were no cars, period. We still had a few hundred kilometres to reach the Libyan border, and not a soul was heading east toward Libya. We hitched at the same spot for three hours with just four cars going by. Each car sped up as they saw us.

"Hitching on to Libya from this little town is frigging hopeless," Blair yelled at me. "We'd be way better off going back toward Tunis, packing it in there for the night and reassessing whether we should keep going to Egypt."

"There is no bloody way I am going backwards," I yelled back. "That's crazy! We are only a short ride from the border, and if we go back, we'll just end up in this damn town tomorrow at the same time. Besides, we would never make it back to Tunis tonight. It will be dark in an hour or so, and there is hardly a car going that way anyway."

We yelled even louder at each other. Then, in a rather dramatic move, Blair took his pack and stomped off across the highway — if you could call a small road covered in sand a highway — faced me, and started hitching in the opposite direction. After thirty minutes or more of us screaming at each other, a car approached, going in Blair's direction. Luckily, it kept going, despite Blair using our manoeuvre of jumping halfway onto the road and forcing the driver to go around him. I jeered and clapped when it passed him.

We stopped talking to each other again.

Later, a car came in my direction. The same thing happened. It just about ran me over trying to get around my rather aggressive hitchhiking style. Blair cheered as the car went by. These were his first words in close to an hour. We were one for one.

It was now almost dark. Blair muttered, "I am going to get a place to sleep for the night and then probably hitch west, not east in the morning." He turned his back to me and walked away. "I have had it."

Dumbfounded and very upset, I managed to scream, loudly enough so I was sure he heard me:

"Meet me in Cairo!"

Cairo is a city of, say, eight million people, but I knew Blair had the name of our recommended hostel in Cairo, a large boat anchored on the Nile that had been converted into a cheap hostel for travellers like us. If he did change his mind, I was certain that's where he would head, and we would be back together.

Stupidly, after Blair walked out of sight, I kept trying to get a ride in the dusk, but there were no cars. Reluctantly, I decided to see if I could find a place to stay for the night in this little town. I was still really upset. This was just a great place to separate. I was in the middle of nowhere and really wanted to go on and see the pyramids, Luxor and the Middle East. There was no way I was going to go backward. I felt very alone and apprehensive about what lay ahead.

I suspected that Blair would head first for a police station, but this was such a small town I doubted there even was one. That would mean he would head for a cheap hotel, but I really didn't want to go to the same one where he was. I needed to do something, since it was almost dark. Even without Blair, I decided to keep going. Undoubtedly, I would meet others. I was convinced he would have second thoughts the next day and hitch to Cairo, where we would meet again.

My French was poor, but after asking a few locals if they had a police station, and if so, where it was, I finally bumped into a small one near the centre of the town I was trying to escape. It was now pitch dark. All I had to do was convince the police to let me stay the night. Who knew? Perhaps Blair was inside, enjoying one of their cells.

Unexpectedly, after examining my passport, a policeman

asked me to get in one of their cars. This was not in the cards. He kept motioning me to the car. At least he had a broad smile on his face as he opened the back door. His buddy got in the front seat and off they went, heading out of town, driving toward the mountains. I was scared shitless, unable to really communicate, stuck in the back seat behind two men far larger than me and not having a clue where we were going.

We climbed into the hills for at least ten minutes, on a small one-lane country road in the jet-black darkness. Suddenly, we came to a large, lit building that looked a lot like an old brick high school built into the hills. The friendlier of the two guys motioned for me to get out of the car and accompanied me to the front door. After he knocked for a while, another somewhat friendly guy opened the door, and the three of us all climbed two flights of stairs together.

They were talking loudly in Arabic, and I had no clue what they were saying but felt relieved that there was a lot of laughter.

They approached a railing that stopped you from falling into a large dining room filled with long tables below. They motioned for me to look down. There was only one person in that room eating dinner: Blair. These guys had figured, what are the odds of two young Canadians being in their town at the same time? They realized we must have had an argument, and after taking Blair to what they now told me was an orphanage, they thought they might as well take me to the same place to see if their hunch was correct.

I ran down to the restaurant, partly because I was starved and very relieved to see Blair. We hugged each other for a long time and agreed we would never break up again.

"I have changed my mind, Jim. It's time to get to that Libyan border early tomorrow morning."

23

Off to Cairo

If your ship doesn't come in swim out to it.

— *Johnathan Winters*

lair and I woke as bosom pals. It didn't hurt that we were both offered long showers and a breakfast to die for by the amazing staff at the orphanage. The border was about 150 kilometres away, which, on a good day, might take three hours. There were only four more days to Christmas, and our goal of reaching Cairo by then looked unattainable. The day started off well, with two short rides and us asking ourselves where these cars were yesterday. Then we were dropped off at a junction in the middle of a desert-like area. I worried we would be there all day again. Right in front of us, a sign read in English: "Cairo 2,500 kilometres that way."

Using our leftover chalk from Marrakesh, I wrote on the other side of the sign, "Vancouver 10,000 kilometres this way." For some reason, this offended a local, who tried to rub out the word *Vancouver* and kept muttering the word "police" to me. Two cars did come by in quick succession, the first a diplomatic car that tried to run us over, and the second a Volkswagen driven by a local whose back seat was piled with a foot of junk and didn't have an inch of room for us. The few houses around us must have had thirty children living in them. They all came out to the highway to stand in front of us and practice their English. Looking at our packs, each of them continually said, pronouncing each syllable, "Ca-na-da."

For the first two minutes, this was nice, but it grew annoying after half an hour. A few women walked by. I wrote in my diary, "They looked kind of scary, with tattoos all over their body, or what you can see of it, as they were wrapped from head to toe in cloth."

Starved and thirsty, we finally went to the nicest-looking house and asked if, by chance, they might give us a glass of water. To hell with bottled water after our discovery a few weeks back. A few minutes later, a kid of maybe five years old came out of his house, neatly dressed, holding a large jug of cold water and two glasses. Heaven. By then, our stomachs had become adjusted to the thousands of bugs in the water, warding off the Arab two-step.

Even though we were a long way from the border, it was time to start walking, because the kids were really getting on our nerves. Just as we started, a small truck picked us up and took us to within a few kilometres of the border. In only a half-hour of walking, Blair and I were at the border, through the Tunisian side and to the Libyan border, where we again watched our passports, containing our precious visas, disappear through a wicket into no man's land.

Out of the blue, Bill showed up. He had just arrived about two hours earlier. Not a car had come by, so we had not missed a thing. Bill had spent a full day at the coliseum rather than our quick cook's tour. Hitchhikers' etiquette demanded that

Bill had a ride through the border before us, since he was there first. But since there were no rides whatsoever, this was sort of irrelevant.

As it was getting dark, the Libyan border guards suggested we sleep under a shed across the street from their office. They were nice enough to make us multiple cups of hot tea, which we drank for hours. Our passports came popping out of their office more quickly than normal and approved. Further, they told us that next morning, a few transport trucks would be passing through the border into Libya. They would make sure we all were able to get rides, so we would soon be on our way. "Why aren't most border guards like these guys?" we wondered.

At seven, I awoke, freezing. There was some commotion around the border hut. There, in front of my eyes, was a guy dressed in a suit, driving a large black Mercedes, heading our way. Both Blair and Bill got to him at the same time, and he said that he would love to have our company, as he wanted to drive to Alexandria, just north of Cairo. It was a two-thousand-kilometre ride from heaven. Not only was the car huge, but our driver even spoke some English.

We jumped into his enormous car, with Bill in the front and Blair and I sharing the large back seat. We were off. All day, I sat in the back of that Mercedes, smiling, while our new friend bought us oranges, dates, fresh bread, cheeses and olives. We drank tea, coffee and cans of Coke. He drove right until nine in the evening, then stopped in a small town and booked a room for himself, telling us he would be back in nine hours. The ride had been fast but boring, barrelling over the flat desert, kilometre after kilometre, often without a road sign. However, we really didn't make good time despite the speed, as he must have stopped forty times that day to ask directions. Without any signs, and with the wind blowing the sand over the road, it was easy to lose what they called the main highway. We were on our way to Benghazi, the major city in eastern Libya, not a long way from the Egyptian border. While our driver slept in the hotel, the three of us just made do with an overnight sleep in his car.

The next morning, our driver told us he was going to veer off the main highway into the real desert, as he wanted to find the Arch of the Philaeni, a marble arch built by the Italians just before the start of the Second World War. Asking directions now every two or three kilometres and heading occasionally in circles, we finally came across a one-hundred-foot-high marble arch jumping out of the desert like a sore thumb. Unveiled in 1937, it had been built by Mussolini as a symbol of the resourcefulness and power of the Italians, who had occupied Libya until the Second World War. The arch, with absolutely nothing around it except desert, appeared far larger than it was. I wrote in my diary, "On the top is a statue of a nude girl. An English bloke during the Second World War painted a bra and panties on her."

In 1969, a few years after we saw the arch, Libyan leader Muammar Gaddafi came to power. One of the first things he did was destroy the arch, since he saw it as a symbol of Italian rule of his country.

Our driver had some business to do in Benghazi, which he found without incident. He parked the car in the middle of the city and asked us to be back in about four hours, which allowed us to do a quick tour of the city. Wandering the city together, we ran across an older uniformed British army sergeant who offered to buy us a beer at his officer's club nearby. It would be a disaster if our driver came back early, as our packs were locked in the trunk, so we made the call to have just one beer and get back to the car a half hour early, just in case. We shouldn't have worried, as he came back right on time, and off we went. As a result, all we really saw of Benghazi was the inside of a British officers' club and a lot of dusty, dirty buildings from inside our luxury car.

Our driver's goal for that night was to make it to a town just a few kilometres before the Egyptian border, where he knew there was a good hotel and restaurant. When we got there later that evening, we decided to sleep outside, right beside the car. After rolling out our sleeping bags in an area that felt soft and comfortable, we fell asleep easily, staring at the stars above. In the morning, we discovered why the ground had felt so soft: it was covered in camel dung. We had failed to notice this little detail in the dark. Luckily nothing stuck to our sleeping bags, and perhaps our choice of a sleeping location was not that bad after all.

It took us just an hour to cross the border into Egypt, which was exceptionally fast. As with our previous border crossings, there was no walking required for the five-kilometre stretch before and after the border. We were the only people crossing at the time, and the border guards had little to do. When they saw a new Mercedes and a guy with money dressed in a suit, there was no way of getting through without some sort of extra payment. The question was: how much? Our new friend was street-smart but realized there was no hope of getting into Egypt unless he slipped them some money. For a while, there was chatter back and forth in Arabic between our driver and the guard, but then we saw them shake hands. He didn't tell us how much, but it must have been considerable, as they were all smiles.

Soon, we were on our way. The highway, which looked more like a sandy local road from the Libyan border east into Egypt, was simply void of cars. It was also without gas stations. Our driver had an extra gas container and knew where to find the next gas station, still hundreds of kilometres away. He was well prepared. With no traffic, we bombed along at 110 kilometres an hour, then slowed to a crawl for half an hour when the sand covered part or all of the highway. We were making good time toward Alexandria. The sand continued to remain a problem because often it would completely cover the road, making it impossible to proceed. Everyone would get out of the car and then speculate where the highway was.

But in no time we were at the outskirts of Alexandria, and it was only five o'clock, Christmas Eve. Our wonderful driver dropped the three of us off at an intersection that led to the main highway to Cairo, as he headed on into the centre of Alexandria. It was a barren area. For some reason, few cars were heading south to Cairo that night. After walking slowly to an area that we thought was a better hitching spot, we saw a gang of young kids walking quickly toward us. They were maybe three hundred metres behind us. As they approached, someone from their group threw a rock, which landed only a few metres behind us. We could hear them yell "killers" in English, which was disturbing. They screamed that we Americans had killed President Kennedy and threw more rocks at us. Now was not the time to stop and try to explain that we were Canadians (well, Bill wasn't, but in this instance, he was a Canadian now). With our packs on, we started jogging down the road, hoping like hell that some car, any car, would appear. If a car came, it would not get past the three of us.

Minute by minute, this was getting tense. The kids got closer and the rocks came more frequently. Then a blue 1956 Chevy came rushing past the kids, and upon seeing us, stopped. Inside were two Navy guys from Britain. We were saved by the Navy! (Only later, when we arrived in Cairo, would we discover that an international incident had prompted this attack on us.)

The Navy guys took us ten kilometres along the road, to the next village, and shared with us a feast of bananas, oranges, cheese and bread. A true Christmas Eve feast. They dropped us off in the centre of town, in front of two small, dingy-looking hotels. They both looked about the same, so under Bill's direction, we walked back and forth to the reception desk of each of them, bargaining for our room. Bill was an old hand at this, and in a short while had a nice large room for us all. He had even lined up some hot mint tea for us all from the proprietor.

The next day was Christmas, and we were in great spirits. The main highway to Cairo appeared to be just around the corner, so we walked for ten minutes to get to it and stuck out our thumbs. Since it was only 350 kilometres to Cairo, with plenty of traffic now, we broke a hitchhiking rule and hitched as a threesome rather than break into two groups.

Luck was with us, because within twenty minutes, a silver Rolls Royce with a uniformed driver stopped. In the back, miles from the driver, was an older English woman, who asked oh-so-politely in English, "Where are you going? Do you need a lift?" She lived just outside of Alexandria, was going to visit her sister for Christmas and would welcome some company. It was even better that we were from the colonies.

This truly was our best ride ever (well, maybe other than the previous ride for three days in the Mercedes). The woman knew the location of our hostel in Cairo, which was a large boat moored on the Nile. Apparently it was famous due to its location only steps from the centre of the city. On the way, she had her driver swing by Giza so we could see the pyramids from a distance and pointed out some of the main sights as we crawled slowly to the centre of the city.

Cairo was massive. The city seemed (and indeed was) larger than both London and New York as we drove by thousands of small buildings crammed against each other, none more than four storeys high. The real difference was the streets. Every one was so packed with people that at times we could only crawl along, in fear of running over a pedestrian. There was really no distinction between where the street ended and a sidewalk started. It was just a swarm of people wherever you looked. On top of the noise from the swarm, every driver virtually lived on his horn. Everywhere it was bedlam.

We checked into our hostel, starved, and started looking for a restaurant for an early dinner. Cairo was dirt cheap and we could get a good dinner for the equivalent of fifteen cents. At these prices, we ate at a real table inside the restaurant with other paying customers. Exhausted from three days of non-stop travel, we almost fell asleep on the dinner table. Back at the hostel, we crashed early and slept for almost twelve hours.

Cairo is almost the end of the hitchhiker's line, unless you are carrying on to Iraq, Afghanistan and then India. The group staying at this hostel was far different than those at, say, a youth hostel in Europe. Blair and I had probably travelled the least of the twenty-odd hitchhikers gathering around for breakfast in this hostel. About half of them were planning to keep going east to India, a number like us were heading for Beirut and a couple were going anti-clockwise, heading back toward Morocco, doing our trip in reverse. Most had been on the road for over a year, whereas we had only been gone from home for six months.

Bill had been travelling with us since Tunis and had been on the road for ten years. Unlike most of the hitchhikers we met on the road, he truly exhibited a dark side. He told us that in Morocco he had pretended to lose all of his travellers' cheques. He then went to the local American Express office, and they immediately reimbursed him to keep their reputation. He now had new cheques. In reality, Bill had never lost these cheques but instead just put them back in his pack. This brought him another four hundred dollars, effectively doubling his money overnight. He could now cash anywhere the new cheques he had just gotten from American Express, but the old ones in his pack were the bad ones. If Bill got caught cashing one of these old, void cheques, reported lost in a formal report that listed their serial numbers, he could end up in jail for a long time. His intent, of course, was to cash the bad cheques later, at an opportune time.

Later that day, in wandered Tom and his Swedish girlfriend, Elsa, whom we had last seen in Tunis. They were surprised that we had beat them to Cairo, since a couple can always hitch far faster than two guys. But then, they didn't get the super ride that we got all the way from the Tunisian border to Alexandria.

Last, there was Ron, whom we had met in Morocco and who had been here for a few days. A confirmed drifter, Ron had been hitching around the world for five years; he hadn't worked for four of those. He explained that he made money the easy way, which meant a bit of smuggling and talking rich men into giving him a few hundred or so. Ron was a nervous wreck who chain-smoked and had lived on ninety cents a day. He looked like a worn-out skeleton, far older than his twenty-seven years.

We had not heard or read any international news forever. As a goal for a lazy day, Blair and I decided to walk over to the British library and see what papers were available, or anything else we could get our hands on. The far more substantial American library (named the John F. Kennedy Library) in Cairo had been burned to the ground just a month earlier by hundreds of students from the Congo who were protesting US interference in their country.

Reading the local English newspapers, Blair and I found out why we had been stoned by the kids in Alexandria. US President

Johnson, who had recently taken over from Kennedy, had given a pro-Israeli speech the night before we were dropped off in Alexandria. In his speech, which centred on supporting Israel, he had told the Palestinians that they could jump into the sea if they didn't like it. Apparently, they didn't like it, and there were riots all over Egypt that night and, of course, in Alexandria.

The next day, we really wanted to see the pyramids, the number one attraction in Egypt and one of the great wonders of the ancient world. We were told to leave early, as by late morning the tour buses would arrive and the experience would not be the same. A bus to Giza, where the pyramids were, was only seven cents. It wasn't worth hitchhiking.

Bill joined Blair and me for the day, and we found the bus station together. Soon we were in Giza, situated on a plateau just outside Cairo. The centre of Egyptian royalty for the kingdom of Egypt some 4,500 years ago, it was known for the three pyramids built there around 2500 BC. To us, it looked like a desert of small rocks broken up by the pyramids. Not a living plant or tree was in sight — just a lot of grey stones stretching for many kilometres.

The twelve-year-old kids were all there, waiting for us. They were trying to sell us camel rides so we could circle the three pyramids and get up close to the Sphinx. Camels were not a bad idea, since the pyramids were spaced out over a few kilometres. It would be neat to ride a camel. But another kid who was selling rides on pure-white horses caught our eye. Since it was early in the morning, he had no customers. We got a good price, and the three of us were soon on our horses, galloping around and around the pyramids. We must have been on those damn horses for most of the morning. In the end, we paid the guy more than we had agreed, having gone so long over the time we said we would return.

It was now time to climb the pyramids. Everyone wanted to climb the main pyramid, called Cheops, which was about 150 metres (480 feet) high. Roughly the height of a fifty-storey building, Cheops is the largest of the three pyramids and the largest one ever built on earth. It was built by the Egyptians about 4,500 years ago to house the tomb of the pharaoh Cheops, hence the name. Over the centuries, the smooth outer coating of the pyramid had worn off right to the top, exposing large, square limestone stones. Apparently there were something like 2.3 million of these stones in just this one pyramid. Each block, about one metre square, was set back from the previous row. The blocks were of different sizes and shapes, with the largest ones on the bottom of the pyramid. The size of the blocks decreased on the way up, but then the situation reversed and they became larger again.

After my vertigo experience at St. Paul's Cathedral in London, I was not that keen to try climbing this thing. In fact, Bill had disappeared and it looked like he was going to give it a miss. But from the ground it looked like the blocks were on a forty-five-degree angle as they gradually came together at the top. All I had to do was navigate my body up and over a one-metre rock, then hop up to the next one. If I looked closely, I could see very narrow paths, where people had climbed along the ridges of the stones. It was not an orderly path but wove its way sideways and up as far as I could see.

It was now noon, and there were more tourists. Not a lot, perhaps a few hundred or so, all walking off their tour buses. We saw there was a little industry going on, with local guides safely taking mainly Americans up to the top of the pyramid and back down for a good fee. Our plan was to follow one of these guides, wait at the top, then follow another guide down. However, I was very slow and couldn't come close to keeping up with the guide, who, of course, was concentrating on his client. Within three rows of stones, about four metres up, I lost our guide. The problem was you had to swing your feet up almost a full metre in the air and struggle to get up onto the next block. The blocks were wide, so once you made it to the block above you, there was no problem finding some space to stand. I thought that if I just kept looking up, there would be no height issue. When I got to the top, I would take one look, gasp and head down.

Although I started to get a bit better at climbing, after twenty minutes, I had only gone a quarter of the way up. Accidently, I looked down. Where was the forty-five-degree grade? It was straight down. Although I was only maybe fifty metres up at the most, it seemed like two hundred to me. When I looked at my feet, I just saw air far below me. (Later, I found out the angle, or grade, going down was closer to fifty-five or sixty degrees, which is getting close to straight down.) Just like at St. Paul's, I froze and could not move. Soon, my entire body was covered in sweat. I thought I was doomed. I couldn't go up and had no hope of going down. One false move and I was going to tumble right to the bottom.

Blair was frustrated and wanted to go up to the top. I glared at him and yelled, "Just go and leave me here to die." A guide came by and took one look at my face, drenched in sweat, and my shaking legs.

"Stay exactly where you are," he said in broken English. Looking at both Blair and me, he added, "I have customer, but will get her up top so quickly. After then, I will bring her down, safely, of course. Then I will climb up to where you are right now and bring you down to earth."

The guide stared into my eyes, wagging his finger at me. "Now, this is very, very important. Don't move. No move your feet. Just stand still and don't look down. I come back. Trust me."

Later, I found out that rarely is anyone hurt climbing up the pyramid, but each year, a few dozen people like me are killed coming down. You have to balance yourself as you jump down to the next block. Many miss and fall to their death. The landing spots are smooth, slippery, covered in sand or loose rocks, often angled downwards, and can be quite narrow or cracked. There were no handholds. Miss just one step and lose your footing, you won't stop tumbling until you're at the bottom.

I waited forever, watching Blair ascend higher and higher. Finally, he arrived back at my level, blabbing.

"Jim, it was just fantastic. I got to the top easily, no sweat, and on top there was a lady over eighty, who had made it there from Boston, who thought it was the highlight of her trip. You should have gone — it was so easy. Well, you might not have loved the view."

To say I got mad at Blair would be a gross understatement. I had pools of sweat all over my body and was shaking uncontrollably, yet all he could talk about was what I had missed. But I was glad he was back, because if the guide didn't show up, I was in deep trouble. I would need Blair to guide me down. I needed to hold my tongue and keep him onside, just to save my ass.

Eventually, the guide did show up. God, was I happy. He took my shaking hand and gently moved me over to his secret path, which wound slowly down each stone with small, safe jumps. We reached the ground in less than twenty minutes. I was so relieved, I gave him a tip of almost a dollar for saving my life. A huge sum.

Bill reappeared and told us there was a nightly light show, in English, which lit up each of the pyramids and the Sphinx, which would give us more of the history of the structures. He had heard it was worth watching but rather expensive. Since

The Cheops pyramid from behind the entrance. Photo by Blair.

everyone had arrived by tour bus, we assumed the same would be true for the night light show. It would be easy in such a wide-open space to sneak into the area and watch the show. It meant we had to kill a few hours until it got dark.

Starved, we walked to a restaurant not far from the pyramids and ate an early dinner until we saw buses arrive for the evening show. We found a great place on top of a sand dune and watched the entire show from there. Toward the end, the bright lights started circling the pyramids — and hit the exact sand dunes we were hiding behind. They lit us up like a candle. So much for our clever concealment.

Our days were spent in Cairo roaming the market, probably the largest I had ever seen, and drinking a lot of tea. In the crowded city, over eight million people lived on top of each other. We visited the Egyptian Museum, but unfortunately, over the years, a lot of Egypt's great works of art had been controversially moved out of Egypt to museums in London, Paris and New York.

As in Tangier, we had a lot of fun watching British and American tourists, fresh off the boat, so to speak, wandering around the centre of the city, waiting to be taken by street-smart kids.

After a quick week in Cairo, it was New Year's Eve. Bill, our leader, had decided that the perfect spot for our celebration was the restaurant-bar on top of the Hilton Hotel. Staying at the Hilton was mandatory to do Cairo in style. The hotel was really a little piece of America: all the staff spoke English, and where else in Cairo could you buy a cheeseburger and stay in an air-conditioned room? Built in 1958 between the banks of the Nile and one of the city's central squares, known as Tahir Square, it was a perfect location. As soon as it opened, it became the new social and political centre of all of Cairo and was still a favourite hotspot. The building itself was an imposing twelve-storey structure, far wider than it was high. Standing out from all the buildings and set off by the Nile, it had been built in an area where no other buildings exceeded three storeys. The hotel represented the symbolic power of the United States.

Bill's plan was to crash the formal party atop the Hilton, which he was certain would be full of rich American tourists and the odd rich American expat. He had even scouted out the place earlier in the day and was confident we could get in. Once in, we would all pretend to be from some city in the US and talk up the friendliest of the partiers, hoping they would buy us a drink and insist to the staff that we stay. Surely, the management of the hotel would not want us out, once our new friends were spending money buying us drinks.

There were now seven of us. Blair and I had become good friends with two Swedes, who were slumming it and staying in our hostel. They had driven their car all the way down from Sweden to Cairo, taking a ferry from southern Italy to North

Africa. Then there was Ron and Elsa, the Swedish bombshell. Bill was dressed in a full camouflage jacket he had picked up in the Congo. With his long beard, he was quite an imposing presence. Ron was wearing his tall black top hat. Blair and I looked rather normal compared to the rest of our group.

Somewhere in Cairo, Bill had found a large bottle of rum. With some sort of mix, the seven of us had a few drinks from the bottle before the real party. The plan was easy. We would just show up, take the elevator to the top where the party was and move in like hell.

Our plan started off great. Bill knew exactly where the elevators were. We marched up to them as if we knew what we were doing and pressed the top-floor button. Our objective was known as the Belvedere Supper Club — very la-di-da. We were quite a sight. Unfortunately, the moment the seven of us got off the elevator in front of the club, we were asked for our tickets. They knew there was no hope that seven hitchhikers dressed like us would ever have tickets in the first place. They quickly put us in the elevator, and down we went to the lobby.

But Bill figured that there had to be a second elevator for staff, where they brought up the food and liquor. There was no way the staff would be allowed to use the same elevator as guests. We fanned out and the Swedes quickly found a small elevator. We all jammed in. This time, the elevator doors opened right into the kitchen.

The kitchen was out of control, since it was near eleven and dinner was being served. This didn't faze Bill, our leader, at all. He grabbed a plate of food that was sitting on a serving table in the kitchen and followed a waiter out into the club, plate in hand. We all tried to find a plate of food to carry and followed Bill, in sort of a conga line, into the nightclub itself, pretending to be poorly dressed waiters.

The club was spectacular. First, there was the view of all of Cairo below us, a long glass bar, and perhaps two hundred formally dressed Americans. As planned, we split up to attack some unsuspecting American and see how quickly we could get them to buy us a drink. We really stood out with our beards and Bill in a rebel Congo jacket. I looked over and saw Ron's large black top hat moving and bobbing as he worked his way through the crowd. Blair and I decided we were from Seattle, a city we knew a bit about, and glommed onto two couples, who smiled at us. After some insistence from us, they decided to buy us a drink.

Our idea worked like a charm for maybe twenty minutes. The only people on the floor of the restaurant were waiters. When they saw us talking to paying customers, who were ordering drinks for us, they did nothing. Blair and I had a great conversation with our two couples, who said they were from LA and were doing Egypt 'in style', as they called it. We asked how things were in the great old United States and mentioned how much we missed home there, all the while hoping, of course, to be quickly offered a drink. All I could recall from my father's drinks was a gin and tonic, so that's what we asked for and got.

But the obvious soon happened. One of the managers, who walked out onto the floor of the restaurant, spotted us. He was not nearly as amused as the waiters, and despite our patrons' protests, we were thrown out. We gulped down our gins and once again headed for the elevators. Just as they were about to leave the bar, Bill and Ron stopped, quieted the crowd and in thundering voices, wished everyone "Happy New Year." We had lasted about half an hour, and it wasn't even midnight.

Now banned from both elevators, we found a much smaller lobby bar on the main floor. We had little money to buy even one drink, but none of us was shy, so we found three older women from America (probably age forty) out on the town for New Year's and willing to buy us all a drink or two. We stayed in that bar for a while, then headed back to our boat less than a kilometre away, where we finished off the bottle of rum we had started earlier in the evening.

The next day, I wrote in my diary, "Today I had a . . . slight headache, the trots, etc., so I stayed in bed, trying to get rid of my diseases."

24

Third Class to Luxor

*Fill your life with adventure, not things. Have stories to tell,
not stuff to show.*

— *Unknown*

Blair and I left for Luxor on a third-class train. Everyone
we knew was heading for Luxor or had just gotten back.
It was time to visit this place where King Tut's tomb was
found in the Valley of the Kings and see the famous Karnak
Temple. Hitchhiking in Egypt was impossible, as the people
had no concept of the idea, and to top it off, there were few if
any cars, even if you could find a highway. Everyone went by
train to Luxor, which was a thirteen-hour trip.

First class was for tourists and local businessmen and
resembled what a normal train would look like in North
America. Second class was a major step down. Only hitchhikers
and the average Egyptian who could not afford first class would
take it. A second-class ticket was only twelve dollars to Luxor,
versus over thirty for first class. Then there was third class. A
third-class ticket to Luxor was two dollars each way — if you
could get one. One small issue was that the operator of the train

would only sell a third-class ticket to a local Egyptian. It was forbidden to sell a third-class ticket to a foreigner, supposedly for safety reasons.

Blair and I made the call to go third class anyway, sure that we could somehow get a ticket. After all, we would save six dollars each way, an enormous sum on our budget. The advice we got from our gang on the boat was that we were crazy to try third class. Far better to use up a few more dollars and go second class. Besides, they said, we would not be able to get a ticket, since it was against government regulations, which we had heard time and time again. Last, a third-class ticket meant only that we were allowed onto the train. Since there were far more passengers than seats for the thirteen-hour journey, getting a seat over the locals was probably impossible.

The best advice we received, and followed, was to go early to the station, since it might take hours to even find where they sold the tickets, much less buy one. The same guy who told us to go at least four hours early said the only way to board the train in third class was to enter through an open window while the train was still coming into the station. In this way, we might have a chance at a seat if we were at the front of the throng. If we waited until the train had slowed to a stop as it came into the station, all the seats would be taken by those who knew the drill.

That afternoon, we took a local bus to the train station at least four hours before the scheduled departure time and started the process of finding out where they were selling third-class tickets to Luxor. When we mentioned the words *train ticket* and *Luxor*, we were directed to a central area where tickets were sold. After waiting for a while, we found they sold only second- and first-class tickets. Again, we were told that as foreigners, we were not allowed to buy a third-class ticket.

Looking around the vast train station, Blair and I saw a swarm of about two hundred Egyptians with maybe five hundred chickens, and kids everywhere, all pressing toward four or five wickets in a wall, none of which seemed open. Surely this was the right crowd for a third-class ticket to Luxor.

The train to Luxor from Cairo was the main train of the day. It simply followed the Nile, so anyone heading south took this one. Luxor was at the end of the road. Since the train started in Alexandria and stopped a bit on the way, when it pulled into the Cairo station, it was already a third full. At Cairo, there would be far more people waiting than seats or space available.

Blair and I ran to this mob waiting to buy a ticket. There was no lineup — just a swarm. A wicket had just opened, which boosted the noise level considerably, as many a local fought to get closer to the ticket sales area. A guy standing near us, who spoke almost perfect English, confirmed that you could buy a third-class ticket for the train to Luxor at this very spot, but he wondered why the hell we wanted to go third class.

With packs on our backs, we surrounded the masses, each of us on one side of the mob. On either side, we were very close to two wickets that had only one flaw: they were closed. Our strategy was that hopefully they would open more wickets and we would be right in front of the line. Everyone around me had large wooden boxes, crates of chickens, sugar cane, sacks of food and clothing, with kids swarming everywhere. Since they were burdened down, they couldn't make the quick moves that we could as options in the line opened up. In one word, it was chaos. All the Egyptians, along with us, had one objective: get a ticket on that train.

We both worked our way sideways into the mob, me keeping an eye on the closed wicket to my right, and Blair on the one to the left. Both making progress, we would soon be standing in front of the still-closed wickets.

Luck was with me. In an instant, the wicket almost directly in front of me opened. I survived the crush of locals now pressing sideways toward the new open wicket. In two minutes, I was in front of the uniformed clerk behind the wicket, asking for two tickets to Luxor, third-class return. I knew the price would be the equivalent of about eight dollars for two of us return and had the money ready, holding up two fingers. I kept repeating the word *Luxor*.

In broken English, the fellow behind the wicket told me that I had made a mistake and that the second-class tickets were sold down that way, pointing to a small lineup two hundred metres away. Undoubtedly, he hoped to get rid of me. I insisted to him that we needed third-class, not second-class tickets, and I would not move from my place, now directly in front of the lineup, until he sold me two third-class return tickets. After looking at the swarm behind me, the ticket guy shook his head, gave me a huge warning in broken English and took my money. I was the proud owner of two third-class return tickets to Luxor. We were home.

Since I had won the ticket contest, it was Blair's turn to get us two seats. This meant climbing through an open window in a moving train to beat anyone stupid enough to try the actual doors to the train car. Our next step in this game was to find out where we should stand on the station platform for the best hope of getting on the train and securing a seat. The train was to approach the station coming out of a tunnel on our left, with the first cars through being first class, then second class, and last, third. By the time the third-class rail cars came through the tunnel, they would be slowing down, as the train came to a full stop when the first-class cars had reached the clean area of the station.

But how would we know whether the train was the one that went all the way to Luxor and wasn't a local train that stopped before getting there? Finding a local who spoke a bit of English, we were told that the Luxor train would be by far the longest train. (This didn't help much because we had no idea what the length of a normal train was.) We learned it should come into the station around five, since it would be leaving at six. We were told that the train would be oversold here in Cairo, then would start dropping more people off than came on as it worked its way down the Nile overnight, arriving in Luxor around seven the next morning. Few local passengers went all the way to Luxor. There was not a single tourist or hitchhiker to be seen on the platform where the third-class cars were supposed to grind to a halt.

It was getting tense, since more of the mob now had tickets and were starting to stake their family and countless belongings along the edge of the track. With a lot of conflicting advice, it seemed our best bet to get a seat was to try for a rail car that was only one car back from second class, rather than the cars at the very back of the train. Although the first of the third-class cars would be moving quickly as they entered the station, and it would be difficult to climb though their windows, in theory, there would be fewer locals making this more daring attempt. In contrast, the cars at the back of the train would be crawling into the station after going through the tunnel, and it would be far easier to climb through a window; however, this meant they would be packed inside.

Blair was fighting off the mob even to get close to the moving train. My job was to look after the packs and make sure I saw which open window Blair dove into. I would run to that window, knowing it would now be a hundred metres farther into the station, and hand Blair the two packs. He would get two seats, and I would casually go through the regular door at the back of the car and join him.

Twenty minutes later, we heard the sound of a train coming from within the tunnel. It had to be our train, since everyone on the platform started to move. Even the chickens in the crates got ready to board. Like sprinters at a starting line, we were in a good position on the platform. Blair watched as the first- and second-class cars zoomed past us, going too fast for comfort. He chose a third-class car right behind second class, which was slowing down to maybe ten kilometres an hour when he started running toward it. In turn, I tried to follow him, running with the two packs in my hands, and watched Blair dive through an open window and disappear. Every person on the platform was running for open windows, but most for cars behind ours.

Within twenty seconds, I was surrounded by Egyptians trying to go through windows in the same way as Blair. But they were too late. I saw Blair inside the car and hoisted both packs up to him through the window. Again, he disappeared into the bowels of the car. Looking at the regular entrance to the car, I saw ten or more Egyptians with all their stuff trying to force their way up the stairs to the back of the car. There was no hope for me, so like Blair, I too climbed through an open window. With one pack beside him saving a space for me, I found him sitting on one of the wooden benches that served as seats.

Blair was in a loud argument, speaking in English with a rather large Egyptian, who was responding in Arabic. Neither of them understood a word the other said. I think the fellow was trying to tell Blair to get the damn pack off the seat so he could sit down. Blair was responding that he needed to save it for his buddy. When I arrived, it became clear the seat was for me. At once, the others around us started to chat among themselves. After a few minutes, I was offered the seat. Blair moved the pack and it was all smiles.

It wasn't easy to get our packs onto the overhead luggage racks because they were crammed with crates of chickens, sugar cane and canvas bags stuffed with clothing. Nonetheless, people just continued to cram more stuff above us. Even a small child found some room up there. Looking at the floor, I noticed a trough running the length of the car exactly in the centre of the aisle. I hoped this was not a latrine, even though it looked like a sawed-off sewer pipe.

The crowd settled down. Two-thirds sat on the wooden benches while the other third stood in the aisle or at both ends of the car. At least they were inside the car. Later on, countless locals clung to the outside windows, grabbing a ride for free. As expected, there was not one North American among the approximately one hundred locals jammed in our rail car. Perhaps ten people had crammed into the space between the rail cars, which was used to walk from one car to the next. Right at the end of the car stood a uniformed policeman with a large gun in his holster. He didn't look like a nice guy.

The train jerked and we were off, only a half-hour late. Within a second, the place was bedlam, with loud conversations everywhere, squawking chickens and kids screaming. Everyone on the train started chewing sugar cane at once. The chewing itself was not bad, but they just spat out the chewed sugar cane liquid into the trough below.

We found out that there were no washrooms in third class, which meant that this trough was going to stink like hell. We had been told, though, that there were plenty of stops en route to Luxor where you could use the bathroom in the station, have a smoke and buy some food.

After a few minutes, our seatmates tried to communicate with us, asking the usual questions in broken English.

"Where you from?"

"Are you from California?

"Where you go?"

In a stroke of genius, I recalled that when I had bought a package of cigarettes a few days earlier, it came with a separate, passport-size portrait of Nasser, the beloved president of Egypt. For some reason, I had taken the small picture out of the cigarette pack and put it in my Seagram bag of goodies. After some fumbling around in my crotch, I found the picture and stuck it to the moist window of our rail car right in front of us. Huge smiles from our seatmates. They asked, "Nasser, Nasser, Nasser — you like?"

Of course, we liked. Blair and I did not have a death wish. They pointed out the picture to their friends throughout the car and indicated me as the one who had put it on the window. This really changed things. Within a few minutes, we had a visit from a guy in the car who spoke far better English than our seatmates.

"Do you know you have made a mistake and gotten into a third-class car?" he asked in reasonable English. "Your tickets are second-class, and it's much nicer, only a car ahead. You should go to your real seats." What he also meant but didn't say was "and we will take yours."

Word went up and down the third-class section of the train that two young Canadians were on board. Soon, a constant parade of younger people dropped by and practised their English. We found out a few rules of proper etiquette on the train. If you got up from your seat at one of the countless stops and went off the train to go to the can or to buy some bread, that seat would always be yours when you got back. There was an honour system, and everyone in third class followed it.

There was a second-class dining car, which was not far from where we were sitting. We told our seatmates we were going to give it a try, to see if we could sneak in as foreigners. It would be a welcome break from the wooden seats of third class, and we knew our seats would still be there when we returned.

We found the dining car and snuck in to an empty table when the waiters weren't looking, since we were coming in from the wrong direction. Ordering some sort of pasta and tea, we settled in on cushioned seats to see if we could make this last hours. Feeling like kings, we stayed there for almost two hours. But our prolonged visit in the dining car was a giveaway. A conductor came by and asked to see our tickets. Once he realized we were from third class, he informed everyone eating, in a very loud voice in an attempt to embarrass us, "This dining car is ONLY for second-class ticket holders and NOT for third-class. You must leave immediately." Blair and I laughed and made it back to our seatmates. We told them, "We did make it into the dining car but missed your company, so we returned." More smiles.

By two in the morning, the ride was losing its charm. We still had another six hours to go. By now, you could really notice the smell. The air was hot and moist, and the stink from the trough hung over the cars. There was no doubt some of the passengers had used the trough as their latrine. Piles of half-eaten sugar cane, mixed with urine, were now going up and down the trough as the car shook back and forth. It was revolting.

We napped a little but good sleep was a real challenge. The good news was that as time went by, more people got off the train than on. With about two hours to go, our car was almost empty. Finally, the train stopped. It was 7:30 a.m. We looked outside and there was the lovely word, *Luxor*.

As with all new places, Blair and I had the name of a hostel or hotel. But arriving in Luxor so early in the morning, dead tired, we had little appetite for starting the process of finding our desired hotel. Instead, we walked across the street from the train station and got a room at what turned out to be a cheap and clean place. We slept until it was almost dark.

Situated right on the east side of the Nile, Luxor is not a large city — everything is within walking distance. That evening, our first task was to find Ron and Elsa, who had partied with us at the Hilton. They had left for Luxor a day earlier than us (travelling second class) and were staying at our recommended hotel. We found them, had a quick dinner together and agreed to meet at the river crossing the next day to get to the Valley of the Kings and Queens.

We had come to Luxor mainly to see King Tut's tomb, but we'd heard there were many other sights well worth seeing as well. King Tut's tomb was on the other side of the Nile, in the Valley of the Kings, about five kilometres away from the city.

The next day, the four of us rented bikes. They had no gears, high handlebars, and a large saddle and looked like they were left over from the war. But they worked. We were off to King Tut's tomb in the Valley of the Kings, where Ron and Elsa had gone the day before. Today, they were going to the Valley of the Queens. Both valleys were on the other side of the Nile. The day before, Ron had made the mistake of renting donkeys to get around, once they had found out how far it was to King Tut's tomb. But they said they certainly would not do that again, since the stubborn creatures had minds of their own.

To get across the river, we had to take a wide barge that accepted any type of vehicle, a flock of sheep, cyclists like us and swarms of locals on foot. Like anything in this region, there were many different prices for crossing the Nile on this boat. The cheapest price was for locals, the most expensive for the American tourist on a guided tour.

Ron knew the price, as they had previously crossed without bikes, picking up their donkeys on the other side of the river.

They had paid the equivalent of six cents a person. However, the boat man asked the four of us for twelve cents each, since we had bikes with us. We exploded. When he threatened to leave without us, we settled on a charge of ten cents each as a compromise. The guy was quite a character. He sized up everyone, except the locals, and charged what the traffic would bear. Being skilled at bargaining and holding all the cards also didn't hurt. After all, there was no other way to cross the Nile, other than a bridge some ten kilometres down the road.

Not really knowing where we were going, and losing Ron and Elsa, who took the turn to the Valley of the Queens, Blair and I asked everyone to help us find the route to the tomb of King Tut. After a false start, we found the tomb, but were aghast to discover that they wanted the equivalent of $1.50 each to get in. To put that in perspective, the hotel room for both Blair and me was fifty-five cents a night. Sure that Ron and Elsa had not paid such a price, we tried to strategize an alternative. Immediately, we noticed that the guy guarding the entrance to the tomb and taking tickets was not the same one who sold you a ticket from a small booth off to the side.

As with anything in Egypt, our thought was to pay off the right person and get in. The guard taking the tickets was the one to approach. In no time, we slipped him the equivalent of fifty cents for the two of us, and we were in. We expected to see King Tut himself — well, maybe his mummy — as well as lots of gold. We began following an English guide and saw a large box that held King Tut and lots of ancient paintings on the walls. The concept was stunning but we were a tad disappointed. The actual tomb was much smaller than we had expected. We continued to see other tombs, all at no cost. Since the vast majority of tourists just wanted to see King Tut's tomb and nothing else, these were free.

As usual, there were lots of scams. One of the best ones was to approach groups of tourists and give them a tremendous deal on a piece of exotic ivory, which turned out to be camel bone—less than exotic. The other scam was selling supposed pieces from the actual tomb. One could pick up an 'original' piece from the walls of King Tut's tomb for about five dollars, a fortune to the scammers.

After three hours, Blair and I tired of the history lesson and biked back to the Nile, where we could board the barge and get back to the city. This is where I learned yet another of life's lessons. The barge guy recognized us as the ones who had short-changed him out of what he considered the correct fare on the way over. This time, he asked fourteen cents to go back.

We yelled at him. "You agreed on ten cents on the way over, so you can't charge more for the trip back. We will call the police!"

He answered in broken English, "Well, you can just wait. Maybe another boat to come soon — or maybe you swim?"

He had us. We had no cards. If we didn't pay, we would not get back to our hotel, unless we wanted to bike twenty kilometres and cross the bridge. From this exchange, I learned when bargaining with someone, make sure you have all the cards in your pocket for leverage.

The next day, we explored the Valley of the Queens. It was not quite up to the Kings, with lots of holes in the ground marking the entrances to tombs and few people in sight. Halfway through the day, we gave up on sightseeing, pedalled back and paid our new friend, the boat owner, the price he demanded right away. He just smiled.

The rest of the day was spent sitting by the river, watching small wooden sailing boats called *feluccas* glide back and forth on the Nile and talking to fellow hitchhikers. We were told that where we were heading, the Middle East, was a bit rough, especially Syria, but Jordan was well worth a week, as the people there were friendly. Beirut would be a total surprise. Expensive, but an amazing jewel of a city, so out of place in the Middle East. Just sitting on the bank in the sun for most of the afternoon was far more enjoyable than trooping around looking for holes in the ground. We enjoyed the afternoon immensely.

The last must-see sight was the Karnak Temple. Everyone told us not to miss it, as it might be one of the greatest preserved temples in the world.

The next day, Blair and I were feeling lazy. Conveniently, the temple was just a twenty-minute walk along the Nile from our hotel. From a distance, we could see over a hundred massive columns arranged in rows. They must have been over ten metres high. The temple had been built in Thebes, where we were standing, the ancient capital of Egypt.

The complex was huge. Soon, we glommed onto an English-speaking guide who was taking the only busload of tourists around the site and explaining its history. We spent the entire morning at the site, but around noon, both Blair and I tired of the history lesson and thought it was time to get back to Cairo and arrange our boat voyage to the eastern Mediterranean.

Since we already had tickets for a train leaving that evening, Blair and I ambled up to the station only an hour before departure. It was easy to get on the train because it was only a quarter full. Most people would be picking it up closer to Cairo. We cased out all the cars in third class and settled on the last car, which was the least occupied, and found some reasonable seats to ourselves. Now prepared for the squalor to come, we broke open our food pack with dinner, breakfast, water and lots of treats. We had everything under the sun in that pack. Our plan was to hold on to the entire bench for as long as we could by

The entrance to the ancient capital of Egypt, the city of Thebes.

pretending to be asleep and hope we would have it all the way to Cairo.

Of course, we were not that fortunate. The train filled up as it passed through countless villages on the Nile. At about midnight, a large group got on the train, about five cars up, and started working their way down to the last car, looking for empty seats. Since it was hard for them to get back to cars farther up, they instead all tried to cram into our car, yelling and pushing with the usual gigantic bags of clothing and the crates of chickens and sugar cane.

I had made a mistake. I realized why the last car was rather empty when we boarded: later on, it would be the last stop for the hundreds of new passengers. Many were trapped in our car for the night. At one point, the policeman at the end of our car took offence with one poor chap and came over and whipped him with the end of his gun.

The next morning, we made it to Cairo. Exhausted and feeling like a pretzel, I slowly walked, one tiny step at a time, off the train to catch a local bus to our old hotel. Once there, I collapsed.

Middle East

he Middle East in early 1965, two years before the Six-Day War. The hitch to Jerusalem from
eirut was short but complex. Our route side-stepped Israel to arrive in Aman, Jordan, from
here we travelled into a divided Jerusalem. Hitching to Turkey, we then took a bus to Ankara
efore hitching on to Istanbul.

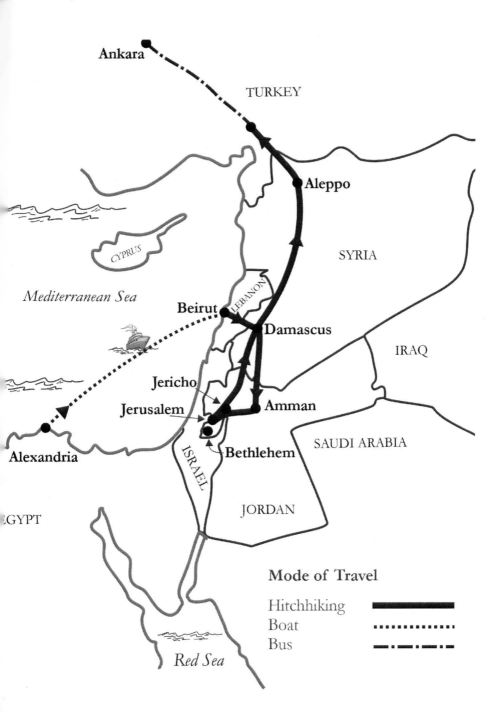

TURKEY

Ankara

Aleppo

CYPRUS

SYRIA

Mediterranean Sea

LEBANON

Beirut

Damascus

IRAQ

Jericho

Jerusalem

Amman

Alexandria

ISRAEL

Bethlehem

SAUDI ARABIA

EGYPT

JORDAN

Red Sea

Mode of Travel

Hitchhiking
Boat
Bus

25

A Delayed Freighter to Beirut

If you think adventure is dangerous, try routine. It's lethal.

— *Paulo Coelho*

Rather than continue on the train all the way to Alexandria, Blair and I stopped in Cairo for two reasons. First, we had been told it was cheaper to buy a ticket for a freighter to Beirut in Cairo rather than wait until we got to Alexandria. Second, many people had told us that Alexandria, a port city, was a dump. The sooner we got out of there, the better. Since we had no idea when the next cheap freighter to Beirut was leaving, we did not want to take the chance of ending up in Alexandria for days. Our hope was to buy a ticket on our day of arrival in Cairo and then take the train to Alexandria the next day. But Blair and I ran across a little hiccup, that meant we needed to spend a few more days in Cairo than planned.

It was impossible to go to the Middle East by land, since travel through the Sinai Peninsula and Israel was forbidden for all travellers. To further complicate things, if you somehow ended up in Israel, you could never get out, except by boat or plane to Europe. Crossing back into Jordan from Israel was also not a good idea, so we were told.

Even mentioning the word *Israel* in Egypt was not wise, so we all used the word *Disneyland* when referring to Israel in public. Everyone went to the eastern Mediterranean by boat through Beirut, Lebanon, and there was lots of advice as to what boat to take and what line was the cheapest. Prices were high. After a few hours going from ticket agency to ticket agency, the cheapest third-class ticket we could find was for an overnight journey on a freighter for the equivalent of fifteen dollars each. We had been told this was the going rate but didn't believe it until we visited countless ticket agencies, each representing different ships. The good news was that once you got to Beirut, you could sell your blood for about eighteen dollars, making three bucks on the deal. The bad news was our boat did not leave for three days, meaning two more nights in Cairo and then on to Alexandria by train. To get a boat for the next day, we would need to pay over forty-five dollars on a regular cruise ship. I would need to find something to do for the two unexpected days in Cairo before we left.

Stupidly, I had mailed my last letter to my parents on arrival in Cairo at the post office without watching them cancel the stamp. I heard later that another scam in Egypt was stealing stamps. A guy working for the post office, who took my money for the stamp, would peel it off my letter as soon as I walked away and resell my stamp for a profit. My fellow hitchhikers thought I was a bit daft for falling for this one. This time, I rewrote the same letter to my parents and demanded that my stamp be cancelled in front of my eyes to prevent him from reselling it to another bloke like me. My parents never did get my first letter, so the rumours may well have been true.

To use up my two extra days, I decided to buy an inlaid copper plate as a souvenir. Blair had decided to use the two days wandering the grand market, hoping something would grab his eye. Prior to leaving for Luxor, I had noticed copper plates for sale everywhere in Cairo. I thought it would be a great item to have to remember my time in Egypt. Depending on the artist, some of these plates were stunning, with inlaid silver depicting an Egyptian god or king from long ago. However, there was no way I was going to carry a copper plate around for the rest of my trip, nor would I mail it from Cairo. So my thought was to take it to Beirut and mail it from there, hoping it would arrive home safely, rather than risk it ending up on the wall of an employee of the Egyptian post office.

The grand market in Cairo is huge. In one large area were all the gold and silver shops, selling everything, including these inlaid copper plates. Attached to some of the shops were so-called factories. These were for show only, to suck in tourists. They might produce one plate every two days, but when I walked in the factory store, there were a few hundred plates ready to be bought. The scam was that the sales guy would walk you through his little factory, showing just how many hours it took to make this plate. After you were impressed with the amount of labour involved, he took you to his show room, asking perhaps ten times more than the plate was worth. Some factories were legitimate, but it took me forever to find a couple of stores that seemed okay.

Once I settled on a store, I found an Egyptian copper plate I loved right away. Of course, the owner told me I had picked out the best plate in the store.

"You must have an eye for things of beauty," he told me in a hushed voice. "In fact, I love this plate so much I hardly want to part with it. No, it's not for sale. I will keep it for my daughter and give it to her on her wedding day."

He paused, as if for dramatic effect, to let this seemingly loving gesture sink in.

"For you, a student? Yes? Well, for you only, no one else, I will sell it for such a fair price, as it would have a good home to be admired by your family. You have a family, yes? It is my treat to you to have the best plate in my store at a price that is below my cost. It is by far the best plate in the market. My best artist in Cairo made this plate."

He then quoted his lowest price, around sixty Egyptian pounds. I expressed outrage and told him that although I loved the plate, there were many like it, and they could be bought for around ten pounds at other stores in the market. The poor owner pretended to faint, then showed me details of workmanship in the plate.

"There is nothing comparable entire market. You will see. Try to find something of this quality." He went on and on.

Finally, he said, "To get the plate sold to the wonderful person you are, I will offer it to you for fifty pounds, final price, but not a pound less. The plate cost me almost fifty pounds to make, and my profit will be only one pound on this transaction. I could not even put food on the table for my starving family at this price."

We went on and on like this for an hour or so. Finally, I got up and said it was late in the day, and I would return after thinking about it. He made a last stab of asking thirty pounds. I walked home.

The next day, the shopkeeper was very surprised and happy to see me show up. I told him I had little time and cut through everything. Could we agree on thirteen pounds? After only ten minutes of haggling, I offered to pay him nineteen pounds, and he finally accepted. We shook hands. As is the custom, he brought out two cups of very hot tea. We sat in his shop and toasted each other with the tea to seal the deal.

After I gave him the money, he told me that seldom does a non-Arab buy things for such a low price, but I had worn him out. I didn't know whether to believe him or not, but looking at what price others wanted for similar plates, it seemed like a good deal.

The next morning, Blair and I did the train thing again but for a much shorter trip, from Cairo to Alexandria. Our boat left the following morning, so we got to the station at six in the morning to make sure we would get on a train that day. Even though the trains ran frequently, we still expected a massive crowd and the usual problem of buying a third-class ticket. Surprisingly, we got our ticket easily for a train leaving at nine and just walked into the rail car rather than using the open-window trick. I guess trains to Alexandria were not as popular as those to Luxor, or else it was still too early in the morning. After an uneventful ride, we soon checked into a nondescript hotel near the port in Alexandria.

The next day, we got up early to head for the docks where our boat was waiting for us. Customs was no sweat. The customs guy just ripped up my declaration sheet in front of me and told me, "You won't need that." Then he burst out laughing.

Our boat was a large freighter that must have been over seventy years old, with rust everywhere. Blair and I watched them load cargo by hand for two or more hours, well past the agreed sailing time. They had just one crane that swung wildly around in random circles, controlled by a hopeless operator. There was constant screaming in Arabic by all the so-called workers below.

The ship was to leave Alexandria by nine and then arrive the next morning in Beirut. This was really the only way to get to the eastern Mediterranean, and the cheapest option available. When we got on and found our beds for the night, it was not good news. Approximately forty bunk beds were thrown into the hold of the ship for third-class passengers. The wall of the hold must have been over twenty feet high, with open portholes at the top. I assumed they were situated just above sea level. Our beds were definitely far below sea level.

Books and clothing had been left to reserve many of the bunks, almost all on the top bunk. We were quite happy to claim a bottom bunk, using my library books to stake our claim, and got the hell out of there. It stunk. There was zero circulation of air. Perhaps we were breathing air from a decade ago.

Luckily, there was a lounge area up above that was probably for second-class passengers, but we snuck in and met two Americans. Like us, they were heading for a tour of the eastern Mediterranean. To avoid the hold, we spent the evening camping out on sofas in the lounge. At midnight, when they closed the area, we were forced to visit our bunk beds.

Blair and I entered a dark hold of stinking, breathing masses of Egyptians. The ship started to toss more and more from side to side. It appeared that not one of the backpackers like us had stooped to go third class. Like on the train ride to Luxor, Blair and I were the only foreigners. Everyone else was in better accommodations above the waterline, in second class. Lying in my bunk bed, I could hear water come through the portholes overhead. What's worse, I heard the distinct sound of one of the passengers throwing up from his bunk. As the ship tossed more and more, I could hear and smell more third-class passengers throwing up. Almost all were on top bunks and throwing up between the beds below but never leaving their own bunk. The fellow directly above me threw up, just missing my bed. I pulled the pack onto my bed and tried to centre myself to miss a direct hit from above.

Within an hour, I could hear someone throwing up every minute or so. The smell was getting worse. It was a boat ride from hell. Our beds rocked and rocked as the storm grew wilder and the boat started lurching in the sea. By now, every time the ship lurched downwards, a mass of seawater would come through the open portholes above to fall on the floor of the hold. Soon, a shallow lake lay under our beds. I thought I saw whitecaps form on our own little lake.

At six in the morning, with maybe an hour of sleep, Blair and I grabbed our packs and headed for the lounge again, hoping it was open. It was, and we passed out there for a few hours, until the guy running it discovered we were third-class passengers and kicked us out. But it was now later in the morning and we moved up onto the deck with all of the other passengers. In the distance, in the now calm waters, we could see the city of Beirut with snow-capped mountains right behind it. It was a stunning sight.

By two in the afternoon, we were off the ship with our new American friends. Beirut was far more prosperous and modern than any city we had seen since leaving Europe ages ago. It could have belonged in Switzerland or France.

On almost every street corner, we saw legs of lamb being barbecued. A street vendor would make a shawarma sandwich, consisting of a slice of barbecued lamb covered in spices, cooked on a vertical rotisserie and then wrapped in warm Arabic bread and topped with chopped tomatoes and a yogurt sauce. After one bite, both Blair and I declared this the best meal in months. During our short stay in Beirut, we must have had five of those sandwiches. They were that good.

The cost of a hotel room was outrageous, and we could not afford our recommended hotel. We were still with the two Americans. Eventually, we all went back to the hotel recommended to them and got a room for the four of us, as they, too, were complaining about the cost of rooms.

The next day, I mailed my newly bought plate to my parents, which cost over three dollars in postage, but at least I had some confidence it would end up in Canada. After the post office, our next stop was to find the place where we could sell our blood for the equivalent of eighteen dollars, which we sorely needed after forking out fifteen dollars for the boat ride. A number of hitchhikers in Cairo had come from Beirut, and almost all had sold their blood there. Some said they got twelve dollars a pint and others eighteen.

It took a while, but Blair and I finally found the place and confirmed that we would, indeed, get eighteen dollars for selling our blood. The building was a bit of a dump. I was expecting a hospital-like setting, but instead it resembled an old bus station waiting room. The crowd was a mix of hitchhikers like us and locals who were obviously down on their luck. Quite a contrast to such places in Canada, where volunteers of all kinds donate their blood for free. But we were not going to chicken out just because the place looked a little rough. There was real money on the line.

There were two lines of people waiting. As usual, Blair and I each chose a line to see who would get to the wicket first. With only five people in front of me, my line moved quite quickly. When I got to the wicket, the woman behind it seemed to have all the severe mannerisms and looks of Nurse Ratched from the movie *One Flew Over the Cuckoo's Nest*.

I could hear her snapping at the American hitchhiker directly in front of me.

"Name — full name, not your half-name. Age. Where you from? Please, now, blood type? You are well — no sick? Read form. You sign now."

Hearing the words *blood type*, I panicked. "What the hell is your blood type?" I called over to Blair. "We need to give them a blood type. By the looks of this woman at the wicket, I could be thrown out of here if I don't come up with one now."

"I am pretty sure it's A positive," Blair yelled back at me from across the room. "At least, I think it is." It looked like the fellow ahead of me was going to move on to where you got the blood removed, so I yelled back, "I will use A positive as well then. I hope it's a common one, as I have no idea what mine is."

Now at the front of the line, I stared right at the battleaxe behind the wicket.

"Jim Kerr, Canada, June 21, 1945, A positive."

I signed a few consent forms and walked over to the chair, where a much nicer nurse sat ready to withdraw my precious blood. Within a few minutes, Blair and I went to yet another wicket with a filled-out form and were paid the equivalent of eighteen bucks.

As we walked out the door, I turned to Blair and said, "I really hope they test my blood to find out what type it is before they use it. I think it's a bit of a disaster if they fill you up with the wrong blood type. They will, won't they? They better." Blair just shook his head. (Later, I enquired if they did check blood type and found out they tested everyone, so luckily my small fib didn't hurt anyone.)

• • •

Beirut was not a friendly city for pedestrians. In two days, we came across just two sidewalks. Crossing a street required more guts and years of experience than we had. Numerous pedestrians were stuck in the median of the road while drivers went as fast as they could in both directions, trapping the poor pedestrians forever. There were no speed-limit signs, and if anything got in the way of drivers, they would just honk. If a driver didn't move his car within one-tenth of a second of the light turning green, every car behind him would start honking immediately. The traffic noise was deafening.

Large Mercedes functioned like a local bus and travelled on set routes around the city. They took up to five passengers and charged little. By a quirk, they were licensed to go from point to point, say, three kilometres apart. They were not allowed to stop on the way and legally could only pick up passengers at the starting point and drop them off at the ending point. If you were only going two kilometres and not three, they could not come to a complete stop, but would slow down to a crawl so you could jump out of the Mercedes as it crawled along. If you wanted to get on at a point along the way, you simply jumped in as the car came to a slow crawl in front of you. These cars were everywhere: cheap, reliable and fun.

Lebanon was a fractured country. About half the people were Christian and the other half Arabic. Added to the mix were thousands of refugees from Syria and Palestine. It was an explosive mix. We heard of threats of revolts, with some bombing thrown in as well. It was well worth keeping alert at all times.

Beirut is built on a point, and the farther inland you go, the steeper it gets as you climb the mountains directly behind the city. The views were stunning. Blair and I toured the American University, overlooking the sea upon the hills above Beirut. Many considered the prestigious university the Harvard of the Middle East. It was at this university that Malcom Kerr (no relation), father of Steve Kerr, the famous basketball player and coach, would later be murdered. As president of the university, Malcom Kerr had only been there for a few years when, in early 1984, in the middle of the Lebanese Civil War, he was shot by two gunmen right outside his office on campus. Apparently, following his father's death, Steve, at age eighteen, threw himself into basketball day and night. Through hard work, he became a star of the Chicago Bulls and played with Michael Jordan.

At this time, Beirut was one of the major financial capitals of the world and the most important financial centre in the Middle East. The rates of exchange from American currency to, say, Turkish pounds were the best in the world. I was fascinated by the different exchange rates and the variety of different currencies available from around the globe. I spent hours with the money-changers and made some purchases of foreign currency at rates better than I would get later on. I loved the money-changing game and enjoyed it far more than going to yet another tourist site in the city.

Unfortunately, Beruit was a very expensive city. We would have loved to stay longer, but we just could not afford the cost of the hotel and food. We made the call to leave the next day for Jordan.

26

Middle-East Politics

I always get to where I'm going by walking away from where I've been.
— *Winnie the Pooh*

Blair and I left early in the morning to hitch to Damascus. As with Alexandria, we had been warned that Damascus was a rough city and not on anyone's list of top cities in the world. We were really heading for Jordan, but to get there, we needed to get around Israel. The normal route was to hitch to Damascus and then south to Aman, Jordan. The total distance we travelled was four hundred kilometres, although a crow could make the journey flying only two hundred. Since we were not crows, we stuck to the highways and avoided 'Disneyland'.

After a few hours of hitching, we were picked up by a pilot of the Royal Jordanian Airlines, who lived in Aman. He asked us to look him up when we got there and took us right to the middle of Damascus, also known as Dams in hitchhiking circles. It was quite the contrast with Beirut and reminded me of some of the large, dusty, sprawling Muslim cities we had passed through in North Africa, but even dirtier. Beirut was full of prosperous people driving Mercedes, with modern high-rises everywhere, whereas Dams was a collection of dirty old buildings and dust-covered roads.

We wandered around the city. While sitting in an outdoor café, Blair and I fell in with a Syrian doctor who eventually invited us to his house for dinner and to stay overnight. He seemed very interested in our views of the capitalist West. We had not forgotten the incident in Tunis with the amorous businessman, but this doctor talked of his young wife, etc., and so we took a chance.

When we arrived, we knew right away we would need to find a hostel for the night. The place was tiny and a dump. It turned out that he was hoping to finish his studies in Canada or the United States through a scholarship. It seemed like he was only a doctor in his own mind at this point. His views of the West were wild. He believed that Great Britain controlled the United Nations and that was why the carving-out of the state of Israel had been forced on the Arab people. He viewed those in the United States as capitalist pigs (I'm not sure how he reconciled this with wanting to study there).

Bitter, he said the mighty capitalist nations of the West were the enemies of the world. The disturbing part? He was far more educated than the average Syrian. Though he was just a sample of one, I was struck by the hatred already engrained in his mind toward the West. As it proved later, he was not alone.

After dinner, we got out of his flat and found the local youth hostel, which was dirt cheap. I think *dirt* was the operative word. The next morning it was cold, and I desperately needed to buy a warm jacket. I was freezing. The city was built on seven hills, a very popular number of hills, like in many places in the Middle East (Fez, Jerusalem, Aman in Jordan . . .). Among all these hills was a market to buy a jacket. I had heard that the warmest type to buy was a sheepskin. By chance,

Damascus was one of the best places in the Middle East to buy one.

After more than an hour of wandering around, I found a small separate market that just sold sheepskin jackets. I cased out all the stalls and found a store with an owner who seemed friendly. With a lot of haggling, I bought a jacket that actually fit me and looked warm as hell. In my diary, I described my payment: "I got it for thirty Syrian pounds, one Lebanese pound, a worn-out blanket I had found in my pack from Oujda, which I had been carrying with me ever since, and an aluminium plate."

It was time to leave. The city was dirty and simply not appealing. Blair and I were seen as wealthy, capitalistic Westerners to be hated and despised. All people from the West, in fact, were seen as supporters of Israel and thus enemies of Syria.

That night, wandering the city, we stumbled upon a movie theatre that was playing a low-budget war movie in English. The war was between England and some Arab nation, and the theatre was packed with hundreds of youths about our age. Blair and I arrived, unseen, just as the movie was starting and scrambled for the last seats available in the front of the theatre. Huge Arabic subtitles took up the bottom third of the screen.

Soon, fighting started between the British soldiers and Arabs on the screen. The Arabs were winning, of course. Almost everyone in the theatre got up from their seats and started screaming in Arabic. When one poor British soldier got blasted by one of the Arabs in a close-up, I thought the entire theatre behind us was going to go nuts. There was no plot. It was just a number of British soldiers getting slaughtered by the Arabs. The more the noise increased behind us, the more Blair and I sank down in our seats, kept our faces down toward the floor and watched from the top of our eyes.

After about a half hour of watching this, I whispered to Blair, "We might have a bit of a problem here, clearly being seen as Westerners like those getting killed on the screen. When we leave, they will turn the house lights on, and we will be dead. They are starting to get really crazy. Let's try and sneak out now, while we are still alive and it's dark, and pretend we are Arabs."

We made the correct call, got up from our seats and literally ran up the aisle for the exit. I think we startled a few people, but no one wanted to miss another kill, so they all stuck to their seats rather than chase us out of the theatre. We had been fortunate to come into the theatre under the cover of darkness. It looked like no one knew they had two Westerners among them. It was another example we witnessed of how much Syrians hated the West from an early age.

• • •

It was time to visit Jerusalem. All of the Biblical sights, including the town of Bethlehem, were in Jordan, not Israel, prior to the Six-Day War in 1967. Jerusalem itself was a divided city, half controlled by Israel and half by Jordan. To get to Jerusalem, Blair and I had to hitch around Israel to Aman, the capital of Jordan, then west to Jerusalem. Not a long way, but with little concept of hitchhiking here, the trip could take a day — or maybe just three hours.

We were pleasantly surprised. Rides appeared frequently from educated Jordanian locals. Blair and I made it to Aman and checked into the local youth hostel for the night. We would have only a short hitch the next morning to Jerusalem. Aman was yet another large, dusty Arabic city and true to form was built on seven hills, but the attitude of its citizens was nothing like that of those in Damascus. They were friendly, asking how they could help us, and we heard the usual questions about us being from California.

We were looking forward to settling down in one place for a while. Once we got to Jerusalem, we thought we would spend five or six days there and use the city as a base to visit the neighbouring sites of Bethlehem and Jericho. But we were not counting on rain and then more rain. After we hitched the next day to a cheap hotel in the centre of Jerusalem, it poured and poured for three solid days. Yes, we were in the middle of a desert, but it was the rainy season. We found that out the hard way. Our hotel was right next to a small pool hall where a lot of Palestinian refugees hung out. We were staying in the Arabic sector of the city (East Jerusalem), since the west side was in Israeli hands, which prevented us from entering. Actually, we could enter, we just were not sure we could go back the way we came and would then be forced to take a boat to Europe. With nothing to do in the pouring rain, it was time to play pool with the local refugees.

Initially, we paid a token amount and Blair and I had a game by ourselves. Neither of us had grown up in a pool hall and we were rather hopeless at the game. Even so, within minutes, two Palestinians approached us and challenged us to a game. Both spoke almost flawless English.

"It won't be much of a game," Blair told them. "I'm sure you've seen how we play, though I must say I'm a bit better than my friend Jim. By the way, I'm Blair and we're from Canada. You probably assumed we were from the US."

They were both bitter and told us their life stories, which were essentially the same. Twenty odd years ago, their families were forced off their land, which they had farmed for centuries. They lost everything. Their parents could take only their moveable possessions from their homes, which were to be occupied by

Jewish settlers. They moved to the Jordanian part of Jerusalem with their families. Since arriving and growing up here, they had had little opportunity for work. Most of the guys in the pool hall were like them and knew no other life than what they had now. Their parents had drilled into them the unfairness of their current position. They begged us to sponsor them to Canada. They had little future where they were now and felt desperate to make something of their life. The reality, of course, was that we had no hope of getting them into Canada. We did take down their names and addresses but were told later that it was a hopeless exercise to try to get a refugee to Canada at that time.

On the second day of rain, we found the American library in Jerusalem. A nice, warm, dry place with recent newspapers from around the world and lots of interesting books on the Arab–Israeli conflict, all in English. We spent the entire afternoon there, then returned to the pool hall to talk to the locals once again and listen to more of their stories.

Over time, I became more and more understanding of their position. Though we did not enter Israel to hear the other side of the story, I found myself thinking: What if I were in their position? What would I do? It seemed that Israel had not been fair in this conflict and had treated the Palestinians poorly.

Jerusalem did have a tacky side. Surrounding every religious site were tourist shops that sold countless imitation gold crosses and hundreds of religious knickknacks. The owners of these small shops would be out on the street almost tackling unsuspecting tourists to come into their shops. But overall, it was a fascinating city and well worth a long stop.

The number one sight in old Jerusalem was the Dome of the Rock, a massive building serving as a centre of religion for both Muslims and Jews and under Jordanian control in the middle of the old city. The Dome was an Islamic shrine built some seven hundred years after Christ was born. Muslims believe that Mohammad's journey to heaven started exactly from the rock at the centre of the structure. For this reason, it is the third holiest site in the Muslim world. For Jews, this was the place of the First Temple. Our first visit to the Dome didn't go too well. Blair and I arrived at noon and for some reason, the Dome closed at 11:30 a.m. that day.

It finally stopped raining on the day we planned to visit Bethlehem, which was located in Jordan, not Israel. Leaving Jerusalem for the very short hitch to Bethlehem, we were fortunate to be picked up by a head guide working for the regional district. The senior guides all drove new cars, and this guy was driving a Cadillac. He told us that before the formation of Israel, the distance from Bethlehem to Jerusalem was just five kilometres driving. Now it was seventeen because one was forced to detour around the Israeli sector of the city. He took us to a hill that looked over Jerusalem, and we could see two halves: one Jewish, the other non-Jewish and mostly Arabic. The Dome of the Rock was clearly visible, perched on the highest piece of land in the centre of the city. It reminded me of Berlin with its clear divide between east and west.

In the middle of this mess stood some land belonging to the United Nations, with their building and troops, trying to keep the peace between the Jews and Arabs. This looked like a very precarious place to be in case anything went wrong. There were no barriers, no barbed wire, just a few military-like buildings sticking out like a sore thumb.

Our guide drove us to Bethlehem and the birthplace of Jesus Christ, now a church. It really was worth the visit, as below the church was the manger. A group of Catholic schoolchildren from Europe were singing hymns, holding candles and burning incense as they walked through the church and down to the manger. It was very moving. If I were at all religious, I would have raved about this experience forever. Later in the day, we returned with our guide to Jerusalem and played pool with our new friends.

The next day, we tried to get into the Dome of the Rock again, but it was closed due to a holiday. Blair and I had a small disagreement: I was dying for a shower, but he didn't want to pay the extra to go to the hostel where we could get hot showers, which were not provided at our hotel. So I left Blair that night and had my shower and agreed to meet him at ten the next morning at, of all places, the Dome of the Rock, to see for the third time if we could get in.

The next day, Blair and I met at exactly the time we had planned: me clean, Blair not so clean. We found out they wanted a fortune to let us enter the Dome. After three days of trying, now we couldn't afford the entry fee. I pleaded with the ticket manager. "You know, all churches in Canada are free, to encourage attendance. If you ever came to Canada, I will make sure you will be charged ten dollars to enter even one of our many churches."

All of a sudden, the manager had a change of heart and said, "You want to see our greatest monument, the Dome of the Rock, right?"

I jumped at this. "Yes, you are so right."

"And you are students, yes?"

"Of course. We are students of the great Muslim monuments around the world."

I have no idea why, but then the man waved his hand toward the entrance, and in we walked for free. We took some pictures of a few devout Muslims washing their feet in the holy water and saw the actual rock in the centre of the dome. Because we conducted our own tour in ten minutes, it was quite disappointing, though the interior walls were entirely covered in mosaics. With its gold sheen, the Dome looked far better from the outside, although we found out the gold was not part of the original design. It was mainly the religious significance of the building that made it famous. Things are not always what they are cracked up to be. Blair and I spent the rest of day slumming around the city and drinking tea. The next day we were off to see the nearby town of Jericho.

I wrote in my diary, "Jericho was nothing more than a large mound of earth with some walls far below ground level. Next door was what was called the Mount of Temptation."

It had been an easy hitch of less than an hour to Jericho from Jerusalem, but we were disappointed on arrival. We did do our trick of joining an English bus tour, learning from our previous experience and in the hope the ancient city could come

People washing their feet before entering the
Al-Aqsa Mosque, also known as the Dome.

alive with a guide explaining the mounds, which looked to be ten thousand years old. In a word, it was boring. However, it looked like you could get a view of the entire valley from the top of a mountain a few kilometres away. About halfway up the mountain, a monastery clung to the side of a rock face. The route to the top of the mountain had a steep but well-worn path that didn't look too dangerous for one with a fear of heights.

We started up the mountain, unaware of its religious significance. Within seconds, two young Palestinian boys joined us. They were a few years younger than us and both spoke excellent English. They had learned English on their own, realizing it was the best chance they had to be able to improve their lot in life. They lived in a large refugee camp that I could now see far below. As we walked, one of the boys told me his father had died in a confrontation against Israel a few years ago. It's hard to imagine what it must feel like if your father was killed by your conqueror and you now lived in a refugee camp with little hope of escaping. I spent most of the climb listening to the boys' stories, which touched me deeply. I wished I could have helped them in some small way.

When we reached the monastery, an old monk showed me a rock where Jesus is said to have sat and met the Devil, who tempted him to switch sides, so the legend goes, but Jesus refused. Hence the name Mount of Temptation. It seemed ironic that from this rock, I could see the refugee camps and a lot of what is now Palestine. After a while, it seemed what the monk really wanted was a donation from me. He never acknowledged the presence of the two refugees.

Before this trip, and before ever leaving Canada, I had had mixed views on the Israeli–Palestinian conflict, but it really wasn't on my radar. After my nights of playing pool with refugees and listening to their stories and the emotional tale of the young fellows climbing with me, I became more and more pro–human rights and pro-Palestine. On the other hand, Blair and I were unable to enter Israel and hear the Israeli point of view. Whether this would have altered my new pro-Palestine stance, I don't know.

From Europe

We arrived in Istanbul by bus in the early spring of 1965. Our hitching route took us to Athens and then to Venice. To get to Venice we had to skirt around Albania and hitch through Yugoslavia. After a short hitch to the major cities of Italy we split up, with your author hitching alone to Vienna, passing up a few days of skiing with Blair due to my inability to ski. Meeting each other in Munich, we hitched to Luxembourg to catch our flight back to New York.

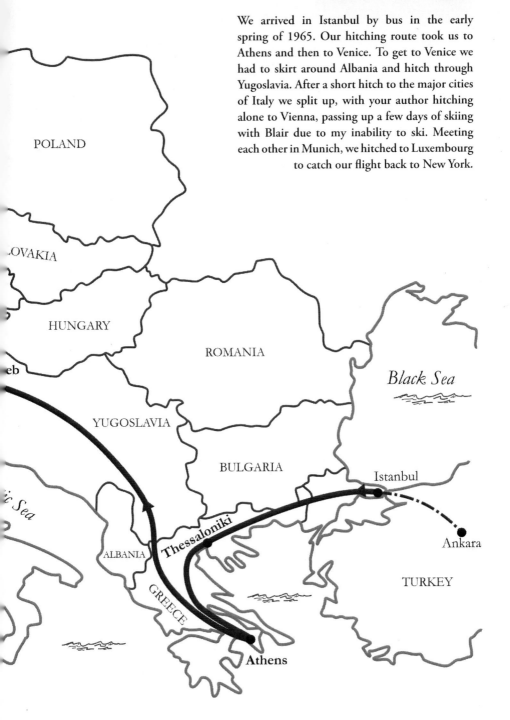

27

Trucker Buddies in Turkey

The traveller sees what he sees, the tourist sees what he has come to see.

— Gilbert Chesterton

I t was time to pull up stakes and move on to Turkey. Not an easy undertaking. To get there, Blair and I had to hitch back to Damascus in Syria, make our way through the city of Aleppo and then south to the border with Turkey. This was not a friendly border, so we needed to be careful. We had heard that the Turks and the Syrians hated each other. The hitching was good, but when we arrived in Dams, something was going on. All the shops were closed, with metal shutters covering their entrances. There was a lot of commotion on the streets, and it appeared there was some kind of social disturbance going on. Few cars appeared on the streets, although we saw a large number of police and army jeeps on the main road, speeding into the city. A well-dressed shopkeeper, who was closing up his store, told us that someone senior in the Muslim world had just been assassinated. We had no idea who he was, but it was obviously very serious. Later, we found out that Hassan Ali Mansur, the prime minister of Iran, had been shot early that morning, January 21, 1965, as he had stepped out of his car, murdered by a Shia fundamentalist group called Fadayan-e Islam.

It looked like the entire country would soon be shut down, and most likely they would close their borders with Turkey. This was not looking good. Of all the places we had so far been, we could not have chosen a worse place than Damascus. We needed to get going now; soon we might not be able to get out of the city due to police roadblocks.

By sheer luck, a fellow who owned a service car, much like a taxi, stopped after seeing us on the main road trying to walk out of Damascus. He told us he lived in Aleppo and was going there right now — exactly where we were headed. He said it was very dangerous to be a Westerner walking on the streets, and we needed to get off the road quickly. As soon as he offered us a ride, we jumped into his car.

Our driver was the first Syrian we met who didn't seem to hold a grudge against the West. During the ride, he gave us a more balanced view of the Syrians but admitted there was indeed a lot of hatred in the city toward America. It rested mainly with the youth of the country, not people of his generation, he said. They had been indoctrinated in schools to despise the West and grew up with a closed mind. After a few hours of conversation about Palestine, the Israeli occupation and the political situation in Syria, he let us off in the centre of Aleppo. It was getting dark, and we found a hotel right away. Aleppo didn't seem as volatile as Dams, but we were still a long way from the Turkish border. Who knew what could happen tomorrow? Our thought was to get on the road before sunrise the next day. The quicker we were out of Syria, the better.

Blair and I got up so early it was still jet black when we hit the road hitching. There were a few cars on the road. After three short rides, we were dropped off only twelve kilometres from the border, and it wasn't even nine o'clock yet. It seemed that those who owned cars in Syria were far more educated than the average citizen and were not nearly as stuck on the concept that we were evil Westerners. Hence the good hitchhiking.

Even so, we were stuck in a poor village consisting of nothing but mud huts. We were the attraction of the week, with probably a hundred small kids following us as we walked through the town, heading for the border. Everyone wore gum boots because of the mud. We feared that these kids might turn on us quickly and start throwing mud balls our way, since we were the so-called evil capitalist Westerners. Getting past the village, we made it to the border thanks to a local bus and a transport truck.

This was not a friendly border. Trucks were not allowed to cross the border from Syria into Turkey. A Turkish truck would wait empty, right on the border; a Syrian truck full of goods would pull up beside it, and all the goods would be moved by hand from one truck to the other. The process took hours.

We had chosen the wrong border crossing. This border was for trucks only. No tourists, just trucks. The border guards told us we were the first tourists they had seen for days, as everyone crossed into Turkey at the main crossing, some forty kilometres to the south. Perhaps it was fortunate that we had made this mistake, because the main border crossing might have been closed to foreigners like us due to the assassination. Blair and I had missed the fork in the road about fifty kilometres earlier, when we were so happy getting our short rides to what we called the mud village.

Since the truck we had hitched a ride with could not cross the border, we walked into Turkey after the normal hassles of having to wait out the guards wanting a small tip to process our passports. Once in Turkey, we flagged down another truck driver, who took us to a small town in the mountains just west of the border, where we waited and waited for a ride. The hitching was appalling, as no one had ever seen a hitchhiker. Slowly, we made our way through a row of trucks and truckers.

By seven o'clock that night, we found ourselves in a trucker's restaurant jammed with truckers, halfway up a long hill, about two hundred kilometres from the border. We had bought quite a few Turkish pounds in Beirut, at a price that beat their official rate, so with money in our pockets we had a great meal with the truckers. Unlike our experience eating across North Africa, we enjoyed sitting in the actual restaurant. The owner spoke a bit of English and took us back to the kitchen to explain all of his great dishes and help us make our selection. Soon a fellow brought out a fiddle and started playing. A few men jumped up and started dancing together to the music.

The truckers soon found out that Blair and I were trying to get to Istanbul, a thousand kilometres away. When we explained that we planned to hitchhike there, they just shook their heads.

"You must take a bus. Cheap, fast and you for sure will be in Istanbul tomorrow evening," one told us in broken English. "You will never make it your way. Turkey is different. The closer and closer you get to Istanbul, the people are not friendly like us. They are mean. You will lose all your money. Take the bus!"

Apparently, the local bus went all the way to Ankara, the capital of Turkey, about halfway to Istanbul. The bus could be hailed down right in front of the restaurant we were in, which was on the main highway to Ankara. There was a great debate among the truckers on how much a ticket to Istanbul would cost. To them, Istanbul was like a foreign land that you might visit once in your lifetime. The general consensus was that we should offer the driver the equivalent of three dollars each, which, luckily, we had on us. We had to make sure we got a transfer ticket because in Ankara we would need to change buses to get to Istanbul. There was really no fixed rate for the bus ride. We were told the local bus to Ankara would stop everywhere, and it would take the rest of the night to get to Ankara. The entire trip would take about twenty hours. It was an easy decision. It saved getting a hotel for the night, as Blair and I would sleep on the bus. Better than taking three or four days to hitch to Istanbul. The local bus was arriving in about two hours, so the timing was perfect.

One of the truckers went up the road to flag down the bus for us. We jumped on when it pulled into the parking lot, and the owner of the restaurant and a number of friendly truckers all crowded around its open door. They bargained the price of our ticket to Istanbul for us, and in the end, we did give the driver the equivalent of three dollars each. Our new friends assured us that everything was in order, the driver closed the door and we waved goodbye. It was a great introduction to the Turkish people. Quite a contrast to the reception we had received from most of the Syrians.

It took twenty-three hours to get to Istanbul, according to my diary. I had never even spent five hours on a bus before, and it was not exactly a pleasing experience. But with every hour, Blair and I moved forward to our destination, Istanbul. It was far faster than trying to hitch from one end of Turkey to the other. There was lots of confusion on changing buses in Ankara. Finding the right express bus to Istanbul and not another local bus was not easy, but we did it.

When Blair and I stopped for food at the bus stops, we were treated like rich foreigners. Charged a fortune for our dinner, we left the amount we thought was fair and simply walked out and got on the bus. However, the owner of the restaurant

was infuriated that his supposed super-profit was walking out
the door. He followed us right to the bus, yelling at us to pay
up. Everyone on the bus knew what was up, that we had been
overcharged, and took our side. Finally, in the early evening,
we arrived at Istanbul and found the American hostel where
everyone stayed. Twenty minutes after arriving, we were both
asleep.

Waking up early, we headed straight for the main post office
in Istanbul, which was the next address we had given to our
parents to mail us letters poste restante.

We stood in line, hoping that when we each called out our
name, the clerk would come back with a letter in his hand. Luck
was with us. We had both received a letter and quickly made for
the outside steps, where we sat in the morning sun to read it and
then read it again. Despite the fact that the letters were from our
parents, we devoured their news from home. It was hard not to
feel homesick here in Istanbul, thousands of miles away. Sitting
on the steps enjoying the sun, we planned our day, starting with
visiting the Blue Mosque, then the Sultan's Palace and lastly
a mosque-turned-museum that had been recommended by a
fellow traveller. We were fortunate that our hotel, known as
the American Hostel, was perfectly situated in the middle of all
these famous sites.

Today was Friday, a big day for Muslims. On this day, much
like our Sunday, the Blue Mosque would be jammed with
worshippers. With no restrictions, we marched into the mosque
and, after taking our shoes off, knelt down with perhaps a
thousand Muslims. As non-believers, we should not have been
there while everyone was praying, but it did make the experience more authentic. We tried to be discreet and stay out of
the way, and we soon retreated to the edge of the building, away
from the prayer area so as to not offend the Muslims.

Istanbul's Blue Mosque, without a doubt the most impressive
religious building we saw on our trip.

This was one of the most famous mosques in the world.
The walls and ceilings were a hundred feet above us, covered
in thousands of brilliant blue tiles. Stained glass windows and
chandeliers were everywhere. It really was an amazing building.
Being there among the thousand Muslims inside the mosque
made it far more special to us.

Our next stop on our day of sightseeing was to visit the
Topkapi Palace, where the Sultan who had ruled Turkey had
lived. The Palace was not far from the Blue Mosque, on the top
of a bluff overlooking the Bosphorus Strait. The palace grounds
were huge, covered in countless buildings, each serving as a
museum that displayed items like the Sultan's dinner service
or other mundane articles of his palatial residence. Our real
interest was to tour the Sultan's harem, but when we found
it, after many failed attempts, they wanted the equivalent of
over a dollar each to enter, to our dismay. We tried our "we are

just poor students" line, pleading, but nothing worked, so we turned around, hoping that the area where he kept his harem wasn't as interesting as it sounded.

Last, we had been told at the hostel not to miss the Hagia Sophia mosque, which had recently been converted into a museum. The mosque had an exceptionally large dome covered in thousands of mosaics. The detail was beyond description.

I spent at least twenty minutes ruining my neck, staring up toward these mosaics. How long had it taken the labourers to build this dome, and who had placed each mosaic a hundred feet above the floor of the building?

Walking back to our hostel, we tried to get our bearings. Istanbul was unlike any city we had seen. Cut in half by the Bosphorus Strait separating Europe from Asia, it is a city where East meets West. To make matters more confusing, the European side was also cut in half by a large inlet known as the Golden Horn. Our hostel was in what was called the old European side, where the markets and most of the main sights were. It was surrounded by water on three sides, and the sights were a few hundred feet above the ocean, serviced by inexpensive trams.

To get to the more modern European side, we had to walk over the Golden Horn inlet on a wide bridge jammed with shops and locals fishing from every spot they could find. The bridge was covered in touristy restaurants, all set below the bridge and right on top of the ocean. The old side, where we were, while poorer, was covered with historical buildings like the Blue Mosque and the Topkapi Palace, as well as the Grand Bazaar. The newer European side included grand boulevards full of rich shops and embassies. In fact, if you were dropped off in the new European side, you might think you were in a sophisticated, very rich West European capital. If you were well off, this is where you lived. The Asian side was harder to get to and quite poor in comparison. One had to grab a local ferry which crossed the Bosphorus to get to the Asian side.

The people were predominantly Muslim, and like all Muslim cities, the wailing of the call for prayers could be heard all over the city. Five times a day, the loudspeakers on the top of the mosques came alive. We could often hear the prayers from two or three mosques at the same time. We had heard these prayers every day since we first entered Morocco. They were a constant reminder that we were not in Kansas anymore. After a while we sort of tuned them out, except at five in the morning, when we just rolled over in bed and waited for the sound to stop.

Over the next few days we settled into life in Istanbul, enjoying the city immensely. It was roughly the same size as Cairo but without the dirt, dust and swarms of people on the streets and sidewalks. To us the main attraction of the city was the Grand Bazaar. We wandered through the bazaar almost every single day. Like the market in Cairo, the Grand Bazaar was a maze of thousands of shops under cover. There was an overall plan to the layout of the stores, with, for example, stores selling just men's shoes all next to each other, another group of stores selling pots and pans all together and hundreds of stores selling Turkish carpets all in the same area.

Blair and I were constantly approached by the shopkeepers, some speaking surprisingly good English. Wandering around the market cost us nothing and was plenty entertaining. The shopkeepers were smart and aggressive and were always trying to entice us into their store in order to get the buy of a lifetime.

The bazaar was always full of shoppers hurrying to get somewhere. There must have been over four thousand shops, scattered in a maze of narrow streets, with only a few entrances to the bazaar. It was impossible not to get lost and it could take a long time to finally find an exit. It was never boring.

I was still trying to think of ways to make some extra money to supplement my meagre funds and spent a lot of time in a shop that sold trick rings. My thought was that these rings were unique and cheap. Surely I could sell a few in, say, Italy at three times the price paid here and make some money. After a while I learned the trick to put the magic rings back together in a few seconds, and after a half hour of bargaining got a fair price. I was going to buy twenty rings but chickened out and bought just ten, hoping that things would work out. Later, when it came time to sell them in Italy, no one wanted them, and I was forced to dump them at a novelty store for the same amount I had paid. My brief experiment in investing had failed.

Blair and I wandered the bazaar and went inside every shop we could find that sold pipes. We were looking to buy another meerschaum pipe, as I had lost the one I had bought in Morocco, and Blair's had broken in half. It took hours to find the right shop, and then we tried to gang up on the shopkeeper to get the best price possible. After a half hour of bargaining, we agreed on a price that was the equivalent of around three dollars each. We thought it was a good price given the shopkeeper started at over twelve dollars. But who knows for sure? It was impossible for us to determine the quality of the pipe.

We had looked at perhaps twenty different pipes before settling on one we thought was a bit lighter than the others. What we were really looking for was a pipe that had been carved out of a block of meerschaum, not one formed from the compressed powder from the stone. The pipes were pure white, and over time, they should turn a deep tan colour from the tobacco. Within weeks, we should both be proud owners of partially tanned pipes.

All the shopkeepers offered us tea. It was a way of getting us into their shop, and while they were sincere and it was their custom, we often refused. This time, to celebrate our purchase of the pipes, the shopkeeper offered us tea and we accepted, not to be rude. Once we gave him our money, out of nowhere appeared a young boy with three cups of tea on a copper tray.

Tea in Turkey was nothing like that served in North America. It was served in a tulip-like, small clear glass. At the bottom of the glass was a dark mixture of black tea, which looked quite foul. Depending on the strength of tea you wanted, they then added boiling hot water to the cup. Milk or cream was never added. You then added two sugar cubes very slowly, one at a time, watching each cube melt in the tea, stirring it until the last bit of sugar had melted. Only then, after waiting a few moments, would you start the process of drinking your tea. Though Turkish coffee was famous, it was tea that was drunk far more often by locals, morning, afternoon and night.

Blair and I soon found a favourite restaurant, and like in Marrakesh, we would walk into the kitchen, examining each of the dishes the cook had going that night, and bargain for our supper. We would choose just two dishes, and the chef, now tolerating us, would spoon out two heaping portions of some meat concoction onto our plates. It seemed every meal ended in another glass of tea, called *chi* or *chai* by the locals. It seemed all one did in Istanbul was drink tea.

Days were spent wandering around the European and Asian sections of the city, crossing back and forth on the public ferry system, which was as cheap as borscht. We saw lots of tourists on boat tours that went up and down the Bosphorous Strait, where one could see all the sights from the water. But for less than the equivalent of ten cents, we could just hop on a local ferry boat, not too sure where it was going, and spend most of the day criss-crossing the strait. We just never got off the ferry, hoping it would go in another direction once it dropped off all its passengers. The Bosphorus was jammed with boats of all sizes, including large freighters that were passing through from the Mediterranean to the Black Sea.

It was February, the rainy season, and some days it just poured for hours, then cleared up for a few hours and poured again. On a particularly lazy day, we slept in until noon. Looking at the rain, we decided that our event for the day was nothing more than choosing a café for some tea, hoping to find a recent copy of the *International Herald* and going to our favourite restaurant for dinner. These long days of doing nothing were the days I enjoyed the most.

We had heard from fellow travellers that there was money to be made selling dress shirts on street corners. We found the Turkish guy who ran this gig, and he explained that he had a dozen or so American-made dress shirts, which he had picked up for next to nothing. He told us that if we sold them, rather than a local, people would be more assured the shirts were made in America. We would be paid the equivalent of one dollar for each shirt sold. There was no reason we couldn't sell twelve shirts a day.

He left us on a major street corner with lots of foot traffic. We had six shirts each. Of course, he also wanted to make sure that we didn't run off with his shirts, and told us he would be back in half an hour or so. He knew where we were staying and didn't look like the kind of guy we should cheat. We chose the busiest street corner we could find and each started yelling, "American shirts for sale." But after an hour, and despite many pitches, Blair and I had not sold a single shirt. We looked at the labels, which were obviously fake. The shirts were not made in the US, as shown on the collar, but probably in a small town in central Turkey. We worried we might be participating in a scam, and a few nights in a Turkish jail was not in our trip plan. So, we gave up after only an hour and returned his shirts when he came to find us. Our solid record of abandoning high-paying jobs was still intact.

Back at the hostel, while I was talking of our stint selling shirts on street corners, a guy told us what had just happened to him a few days before we arrived. Two English blokes had successfully sold shirts for the same guy for two days and made a few bucks. However, on the third day, they didn't come back to the hostel. Apparently, they had been caught by the police, given a fine and had to spend the night in jail. They were booted out of the city the next day with a threat of more jail time if they returned. They had rushed back to the hostel to get their stuff and had said it scared the hell out of them. We had escaped a disaster.

After an enjoyable week in Istanbul, it was time to leave for Athens. Getting there would not be easy, as the Greeks and Turks also hated each other, making this border crossing difficult as well. The day before Blair and I left, we spent the day washing our clothes and cleaning up everything. It helped that it rained all day, so we spent the day playing cards and learning more about Athens. Blair thought he had struck gold with his pen pal in Athens and her friend, both young models who were apparently looking forward to meeting us.

The next day was the end of Ramadan, a roughly thirty-day period for all Muslims to practise self-restraint. From dawn to dusk, Muslims cannot eat food, drink, smoke or have sex. Further, they cannot do anything that might be considered immoral; even unintended immoral thoughts are forbidden. On the first day of Ramadan, we had been in Egypt and had dealt with this religious observance ever since. Though the rules did not apply to us, we were very careful to follow them and not offend the local Muslims. Our breakfasts were always in our hostel or just grabbing some bread out of their sight. Lunch was almost always some bread or fruit that we could eat in some dark corner. No sex was no problem for us, of course. By the time Blair and I had dinner, it was dark and everyone was eating, since the fast for that day was over. One day, without thought, we did have a cigarette in front of some locals, who were all addicted and unable to smoke till dusk, when the whole city lit up at once. As we smoked, the locals were unable to take their eyes off us. It was a mistake not to be repeated.

The end of Ramadan was celebrated with an all-night feast. The whole city would celebrate, and it seemed well worth it to put off our departure by just one day. There would be no such celebration in Greece. The next day, however, we were disappointed. The feast was all within large families at full restaurants. There was no inclusion in these celebrations for non-Muslims like us.

28

Athens

You can waste your life drawing lines. Or you can live your life crossing them.

— *Shonda Rhimes*

We left Istanbul early the next day, taking a local bus to get out of the city toward the border with Greece. It took us just four uneventful days of hitchhiking to make it to the centre of Athens, home of what we thought would be our best pen pals ever.

Arriving at our hotel, which many had recommended, Blair phoned Evelyn, his dream pen pal, and received instructions on how to find her apartment. We had the address from her last letter, but even with her instructions, it took over three hours to find her apartment. Understandably, the street signs were written in Greek, and so the address in English was of little help. Blair and I were surprised how few people spoke English. We must have asked a dozen locals where the address was before being pointed in the right direction. When we seemed to be going in circles, Blair told me he really didn't understand a word Evelyn had said on the phone, as her English was somewhat rudimentary.

We eventually made our way up a series of stairs to a tiny, cramped apartment where Evelyn, her brother and her parents were waiting for us. Formally dressed in what looked like a very expen-sive skirt and high heels, Evelyn looked just like her photo, and we could see why she was a budding model. As soon as we arrived, they all politely shook our hands, which was a bit unusual.

Yassas was their first word to us, which must mean "hello."

We repeated the word, again and again, to much laughter. After the success of the hellos, we tried a bit of English, telling them we'd had a little trouble finding their place, as everything was in Greek (our attempt at a weak joke). This was met by puzzled looks. No laughter. We could also see why there was no invitation for Blair and me to stay at their apartment, unless we were prepared to sleep under the dinner table.

Evelyn's father was intent on making sure his guests were served some Greek coffee. He was a short, very happy man with a great smile, and he set about making us all a coffee once he had figured out that we were both saying yes to his request. We watched him take a small copper pot with a wooden handle from a shelf. With great care, he filled it with a finely ground black coffee, water and some sugar and set the pot on the small stove. With a grin, he poured coffee for both Blair and me into two espresso-type cups and then poured for his family. Watching us intently, he took a loud slurp of coffee and we did the same, to much laughter. Not understanding each other really wasn't going to be a problem — and might even be a lot of fun.

Evelyn had phoned her good friend Ecole, also an aspiring model, to come over and meet us. But there was one flaw. Evelyn spoke English so slowly and deliberately that I almost went to sleep during her answer to one of Blair's excited questions. When Ecole arrived, it appeared her English was the same, or perhaps even worse, but still a lot better than our Greek. Nevertheless, it was agreed that tomorrow they would show us all around Athens, starting with the famous Acropolis. Blair and I were to meet them at the apartment around eleven o'clock the next morning. Things were looking up. We slowly finished our coffee and left, as Blair quite uncharacteristically said he was a bit tired.

The next morning, there was a little hiccup. Blair confessed that he had a rather ugly boil growing in his armpit and was in much pain. It had been hurting a lot the previous night. He didn't want to dwell on it, but that's why he had wanted to leave early. I took a look but had to turn away, as it looked so bad. Larger than the size of a golf ball, it looked evil. I asked him if we should go ahead on our tour of Athens or maybe go to a doctor instead, but Blair claimed it really wasn't that bad.

We left to meet Evelyn and Ecole, and five of us set off to climb the hills leading toward the Acropolis (Evelyn's younger brother had invited himself along). Blair and I were dressed in our typical uniforms: very old pants and torn sweaters. Despite the climb, the girls were dressed in skirts and shoes with small heels. It was quite the contrast in fashion statements.

We spent most of the day on the Acropolis, a giant rock high above the city, on which the Parthenon was built. It's right in the centre of Athens and visible from everywhere. The Parthenon, the icon of Western architecture, with multiple Greek columns, was built in the fifth century. We knew nothing about it and were keen to find out more, so we employed our usual strategy of following an American tour bus group with an English-speaking guide. But with the average age of the tour group being in the seventies, our youthful faces stood out like a sore thumb, and we were soon asked to leave. Luckily, there were many information plaques in English, and we were able to learn a lot about the ancient Greeks. The Parthenon was a former temple dedicated to the goddess Athena, whom the people of

Our model pen pals, Ecole on the left of me, Evelyn on the right,
and the ever-present younger brother on top of the Parthenon.

Athens considered their patron. She symbolized wisdom, arts, and culture.

After spending most of the afternoon on the Acropolis, we walked down to a hip bar in the Plaka, an area with narrow streets and, much like a medina in Morocco, brimming with small coffee bars, restaurants and shops. Perhaps a bit touristy, but built on the hill, so there were views of the city from everywhere. Blair and I noticed that the younger brother seemed to be stuck to the girls like glue.

Later in the evening, we took all of them to dinner in a small restaurant they knew in the Plaka. Even though Athens seemed cheap for Europe, it was probably three times the cost of a similar dinner in the Middle East. In an effort to build up some chemistry with Evelyn, Blair thought he would try a bit of conversation over dinner.

"How . . . are you . . . doing tonight . . ., Evelyn?"

A long pause. "Fine."

Blair continued. "Do . . . you like . . . this . . . restaurant?"

A longer pause. "I . . . like . . . this place . . . very . . . much. Thank you, . . . Mr. Blair."

"What is the name of the drink you ordered?"

A longer pause than normal. "I . . . don't . . . know the name, Mr. Blair, in English . . ."

The entire evening continued this way, until Blair gave up and we went back to our hostel.

The next morning, Blair's boil was worse. I could hardly look. It appeared infected. With little money, going to a doctor was an issue. However, dying of an infected boil in Greece didn't seem like a good option, so we both went to the Canadian consulate in Athens for a recommendation of a local doctor. They recommended one who could see Blair late that afternoon after all his scheduled appointments.

I waited outside the doctor's office while the doctor confirmed my suspicions. The boil was close to being infected, and he told Blair that it needed to be lanced. However, before he could do the lancing, Blair would need to spend the next twenty-four hours putting hot compresses directly on the boil. He was given a prescription for some drugs and told to come back to the office in two days for the procedure.

That night, we had agreed to meet the girls at a different bar in the Plaka. A little boil was not going to deter Blair. After a few souvlakis for dinner, cooked right on the sidewalk, we found the bar right on time, but the girls were not there. We later learned that when someone in Greece says they will meet you at ten o'clock, they really mean ten-thirty or even eleven. It was rude to show up right on time. True to form, forty-five minutes after Blair and I had nursed the cheapest beer in the house, the girls arrived, again with Evelyn's brother.

It was more fun this time, more relaxed than dinner the previous night. Blair had almost given up trying to ask Evelyn more questions. Instead, we began to communicate with hand signals and facial expressions. Little by little, we found that the younger brother's English was superior to that of the girls. So, late in the evening, all our conversations went through Evelyn's brother, who was pleased to be the centre of attention. We even tasked him with ordering the last round of drinks. We had discovered that in Greece, young women did not go out alone on a date without a chaperone. We rarely saw a couple out alone on a date. Everyone went out in groups of at least five or six.

During a lull in the conversation, I asked Ecole how she liked modelling, and she actually understood the question. She told me she loved it, though gigs were few. They paid for her evenings at bars and night clubs, which she apparently loved.

It appeared that the centre of life for both girls was night clubs and modelling assignments — certainly a different life than Blair and I had lived for the last eight months.

The next morning we were up early, with Blair in pain and me wondering what to do. It was the boil versus the girls, and it looked like the boil was going to win this time. Reluctantly, Blair decided to follow the doctor's orders and hang around the hotel all day, putting hot compresses on the boil, taking his drugs and resting. He didn't seem to appreciate my jokes, such as "Looks like things are boiling over between you and Evelyn."

I thought it would be a good day to get a paper, find a small café for a coffee, spend a few hours watching the scene and read the paper from start to finish. It was easy to find a paper, because the *Herald Tribune* international edition was found in almost every newspaper stand, hidden behind the local papers. Since it was published once a week, I would never know when I bought the paper if the news was current or a week old. But it really didn't matter. Finding a suitable coffee shop was a harder task. First was the matter of cost. The café had to be off the normal tourist track. Second, to watch the action, I wanted a café that would look onto a small square.

After walking kilometres through the Plaka, I stumbled upon the perfect café. I found a small table overlooking the square, opened my paper and looked around. Like all coffee shops in Athens, there were no women to be seen inside. I could have gotten a coffee for less money standing at the bar but would have been unable to read my paper. Since I was a foreigner, the waiters ignored me, but that suited my purpose of staying as long as I could to read my paper. I was in no hurry to track down a waiter. They wouldn't come within three metres of my table unless they had to walk by to reach someone else, then they would turn their heads to avoid eye contact. Locals would arrive, order their coffee and be served while I just continued to read my paper without my coffee.

After thirty minutes, the waiters realized I was not moving and approached my table. I ordered a coffee similar to the one we had been served by Evelyn's father. I was tempted to order a frappe, a new sensation in Athens, which was Nescafe coffee with sugar, milk and water, but it would be twice the cost, and I was already splurging.

I thought of how many times Blair and I had sat at a small café, drinking a coffee or tea and watching the world go by. Sometimes we borrowed a paper, and other times, feeling flush, we bought one. My first experience hanging out forever in a café was in Tangier, where the highlight was watching the new tourists get taken by the locals. From there I spent hours in cafés reading a paper in Marrakesh, Tunis, Cairo, Jerusalem, Istanbul and now Athens. Back home in Kelowna, they had not even heard of the concept of a café that served coffee.

Sitting there, alone, I thought of what I was going to do with my life upon my return to Canada. Engineering was out. I had really enjoyed dealing with the money-changers in Beirut and thought perhaps I might have some talent in that direction. It seemed that changing faculties to Commerce might be the way to go, leading to an investment business or banking. Contemplating life at the café that day did lead to my enrollment in Commerce at UBC. After working as a stock trader for a summer, I changed career direction and eventually got my chartered accountant degree, leading to a long career and partnership with a large CA firm.

When I got back to the hostel, Blair was in considerable discomfort and though hungry, had no desire to leave the room. We decided to eat in that night, with me scouring stores for the gourmet meal that Blair deserved, but on the budget of a squirrel. I bought a few shish kebabs, gained from a local guy cooking on the sidewalk behind our hotel, some additional bread, cheese and masses of fresh tomatoes. To top it off, I found a bottle of cheap white wine, called retsina, which was a Greek staple.

On my return, Blair was far happier, especially on seeing the wine, but when he tasted it before I had a chance, he spat it out on the floor.

"What a wonderful wine, you got. Jesus, the bloody stuff tastes like turpentine. No wonder you got it so cheap."

I tasted the wine and had to agree. I had made a bad choice. But despite the taste, Blair and I finished the bottle. Blair told me we had been invited to Evelyn's parents', together with Ecole, the next night for dinner at eight. We agreed we should arrive perhaps around nine and went to bed early.

The next day, I went with Blair to the doctor for the lancing. A half hour later, he appeared from the doctor's office in a good mood, with masses of bandages to use later. All had gone well.

"How, by the way, are you handling the payment problem?" I asked Blair.

"Well, I convinced the doctor that through dad's employment in Canada, I had some really great insurance that was good around the world. So, he said he would settle the bill on my last visit and take my insurance to pay for it. Can you believe it? I really have no idea if the insurance will cover me out of Canada, but it's worth a try. I gotta return to make sure the boil has healed over and is not infected. You know, the damn thing already feels better. You should have seen how much liquid came out of the bloody thing when he lanced it. Must have been a cupful!"

We arrived almost an hour late for dinner, bringing with us the second cheapest white wine we could find after retsina. I could tell our late arrival time was correct, as Evelyn's mother was still slaving over the stove as we arrived. She must have spent all day cooking dinner.

The seven of us (the brother was there, of course) sat down at the crowded table that sat five. We were presented with at least eight separate dishes. I could recognize a few, including fried calamari, a huge bowl of fresh tomatoes mixed with onions, some sort of eggplant dish with meat inside and a flat, fried-cheese concoction. Blair and I were in heaven and perhaps ate too many platefuls. The tomatoes were out of this world. We were surprised to find that this was not the entire meal. After the mother had taken all of the dishes off the table, she then took a massive dish of moussaka out of the oven, which we struggled to finish. To top things off, Evelyn's father poured us all a glass of ouzo, a licorice liquor that I choked on. It seemed to be straight alcohol.

Evelyn's parents told us stories of the German occupation of Athens during the Second World War. A giant Nazi flag was flown at the top of the Acropolis, visible throughout the city. One day, the citizens looked up and instead of the Nazi flag, they saw the flag of Greece. Some bold soul had replaced the flag in the dead of night, risking their life. The occupation of the city was a dreadful time and still on the mind of her father more than two decades later.

These stories took a long time to tell, since the conversation was directed to their young son, who in turn tried to translate the Greek into English. It was a bit of comedy as Blair and I, in turn, replied by speaking directly to Evelyn's brother. He, in turn, would tell the parents in Greek what we had said. The turnaround time from parents to brother to us and then back to brother and to parents sometimes took two or three minutes, before laughter was heard at the other end of the table.

At one point, Blair and I casually mentioned that we had just arrived from Turkey. We had forgotten that the Greeks and the Turks hated each other. Her father gave us a short lecture on avoiding Turkey at all costs. After a series of translations, we confessed that visiting Turkey was a mistake and immediately told the table how fabulous Greece was and that our favourite city, by far, was Athens.

It was a wonderful evening. For Blair, the best part of the evening was that Evelyn asked if we wanted to meet them again for lunch at a restaurant they knew just outside the Plaka. We jumped at the invitation, of course, and went home happy.

The next day, once again, we paid for lunch for the five of us in a rather upscale restaurant that Blair and I would never have chosen on our own. From there, we spent all afternoon seeing a grittier and more interesting part of Athens than the Plaka.

On the way to our hotel, I told Blair that we couldn't keep buying drinks and dinners. In a week, we would have nothing left. We needed to either make some more money or get the hell out of Athens.

Blair and I on the top of the Acropolis, overlooking the city of Athens. Note the author's posture and demeanour. Quite a contrast to the picture of Jim with his head down at the very start of our trip.

By chance, we heard that we could also sell our blood in Athens, much like in Beirut. The only issue was you were supposed to wait six weeks before selling your blood again. It was only a month, at best, since Blair and I had sold our blood in Beirut. We found the blood shop, to give it a name, and decided we should sell two-thirds of the amount we sold in Beirut, just to be careful. We were paid the equivalent of ten dollars each, which was a major boost to our finances. Here in Athens, we were spending five dollars a day, rather than our usual two or three. With our newly gained 'blood money', we could finance two more days in Athens. Later that day, I explained to the girls that we were going to have to move on soon. I told them that visiting them was the highlight of our trip, but I was thinking to myself that we would be in a loop forever. Spend money on the girls, sell more blood, take the girls out, sell more blood, etc.

The next day, Blair received the good news that the boil had, indeed, healed and was not infected. Even better news was that the doctor did accept his Canadian insurance. He had presented Blair with a bill of about forty-five dollars: a fortune for us. I am sure that doctor is still waiting to be paid. I have assurances from Blair that if the doctor is still alive today, he will wire over the forty-five dollars immediately.

Although we had been in Athens longer than anticipated, Blair said to me that night, "Let's try just one more night with the girls, okay, Jim? Maybe I can find a way to ditch the brother as the night wears on. If this night ends like all the others, then I agree, it's time to move on."

Reluctantly, I agreed.

We asked the girls to do the night club routine again, avoiding dinner and agreeing to meet them at their favourite bar at ten, meaning 10:45. Again, the younger brother stuck with us. Although Blair and I had a great evening, we returned to our hotel at two o'clock in the morning alone. It was game over.

We were very happy that we saw a lot of Athens beyond the standard tourist places that no one else would see, and we enjoyed being with two beautiful women, but it was time to leave.

At the start of our trip, we had arranged for an open ticket with Icelandic Airlines from Luxembourg to New York. Fortunately, Icelandic Airlines had an office in Athens, which gave us an opportunity to get our return ticket, as long as we could figure out the date of departure. The next day, our last in Athens, I thought we should go over our funds on hand, our budget and how many days we could last before jumping on the plane.

I suggested to Blair that we go to my café of a few days ago and, over a long coffee, work out exactly when we should fly home and make a rough plan for the remaining days of our trip. On the way to the café, I couldn't help but notice the whiteness of everything. If your favourite colour is white, you would love Athens. The whitewashed buildings provided the perfect contrast to the bright blue sky and the colourful flowers that covered the doors and windows of the well-kept homes.

It took us a few hours over coffee to set March 13 as our departure date. This meant we had just twenty-four days left before we hopped on our plane home. We set the date after figuring out how much money we had left and what we still wanted to see. Our plan was to see sights in some of the major cities of Italy. Unfortunately, we were a long way from that country. To get there, we would have to hitch around Albania and through all of Yugoslavia: a distance of a whopping two thousand kilometres. After Italy, we would head to the beer halls in Munich and then do the short hitch to Luxembourg to catch our plane.

Blair then suggested something that was not in the plan. He was keen to spend three or four days at a ski resort in northern Italy for students. He would fit this in before we went to Munich to end our journey. His parents had agreed to lend him the extra funds for this adventure. I was not keen on this because I had never skied in my life, and the southern Alps didn't sound like the best place to start. I doubted they had many bunny hills.

Easily finding the Icelandic Airlines office, set on Syntagma Square, the main square in central Athens, we left with tickets in hand for our departure on March 13. We hoped to get to Italy more quickly than expected, to allow us some time to see the country. It was time to get back to our hostel and spend the rest of the day washing our clothes and cleaning up our packs, which were a mess.

29

Home

Travel isn't always pretty. It isn't always comfortable. Sometimes it hurts, it even breaks your heart.

But that's OK. The journey changes you; it should change you. It leaves marks on your memory, on your consciousness, on your heart, and on your body. You take something with you. Hopefully, you leave something good behind.

— *Anthony Bourdain*

I walked into the Munich Hofbräuhaus alone. Blair had decided, after all, to take off skiing for a few days. I had left him just north of Pisa, where he went northeast and I went north to Vienna. He was expected to be in Munich the next evening. That left us two more days in Munich and then to Luxembourg to catch our plane to New York and hitch home.

We had made a rookie error in not leaving enough time to properly see Italy, partly because we were running out of money and partly because we underestimated how long it would take to hitchhike there from Athens. Our tour of Italy was like one of the famous bus tours for the older folk, where you spent two nights in each city, pretending you had done that city, and moved on to the next. It had been far too much of a rush. We had broken the basic rule of spending enough time in a city to know it well and then move on, rather than staying just long enough to see two or three of the main sights and then get the hell out of there as quickly as possible.

As soon as I walked through the giant doors of the Munich beer hall, I felt at home. What a beer hall, with seating for maybe seven hundred people or more, an oompah band playing all day and long tables of drinkers with litre mugs of beer in front of them. Everyone sat at long tables, crammed together, so it was easy to start a conversation and make friends, especially after a couple of one-litre mugs of beer. It seemed like just one tune, the popular German drinking song "Ein, Zwei, Sofa" ("One, Two, Chug") was played over and over again by the band, with the chorus sung over and over. That night, I closed the place down, meeting a lot of Californians my age who were on a tour of Europe. After a few hours with many a beer, we all became fast friends.

The night before, I had hitched to the centre of Munich and checked in at the local youth hostel. That morning, I had grabbed a 'late' breakfast (*late* meant nine thirty; the hostel's rule number 41 stated that you had to be out of the hostel by exactly ten). Heading out to see some of the city, I had stumbled upon the old town of Munich, full of historic buildings and monuments, most of which had escaped damage from the Second World War. I bumped into a town square that featured a massive town hall, built in, believe it or not, Gothic style. I was by now an expert in Gothic architecture. Spending a few hours just on this square, I nursed a coffee and, of course, read the latest copy of the *International Herald*. It was a very enjoyable day walking the streets, only topped off by my visit to the Hofbräuhaus.

The next day, Blair hadn't make it to the hostel, so I went out to grab a cheap dinner on the sidewalk somewhere. I left a note telling him I would be spending the evening at the Hofbräuhaus with my new long-lost bosom friends. On perhaps my third visit to the loo at the beer hall, I happened to look sideways at the urinal and there was Blair — right beside me!

What a way to meet. I brought Blair back to our table. He went on and on about the skiing and how I had missed the highlight of the trip.

Munich was a wonderful city, but Blair and I had only one day left before hitching to Luxembourg and then flying home the next day. Over breakfast in the youth hostel, we sat beside a guy from the US who had just visited the Dachau concentration camp. He strongly advised us not to miss it. A new presentation centre had been built and opened a few months ago, and it would blow our minds.

We instantly decided to hitch to Dachau that morning instead of seeing more of Munich. It was only fifteen kilometres north of the city. The hitch to Dachau was quick and uneventful, though we had to walk the last few kilometres to the presentation centre.

Entering the newly constructed centre, we were overcome by the large black-and-white pictures of thousands of prisoners, dressed in rags, jammed into the barracks of the concentration camp. Dachau started as a forced-work concentration camp in the mid 1930s for political prisoners who were against the Nazi regime and Hitler. As time went on, thousands of German Jewish prisoners were taken in trains to the camp. The photos depicted men that were half alive, weighing less than a hundred pounds. Their faces were blank.

We were able to walk through part of the camp, which had been reconstructed, including two of the original crematoria, where thousands of bodies had been burned. The camp itself was over twenty acres, but only a quarter of the space was used to house up to thirty thousand prisoners at a time. Surrounded by seven watchtowers manned by guards, a giant fence, a moat and last, an electric fence, it was impossible to escape. The prisoners were forced to work seven days a week making ammunition for the Nazis. With little food, many simply starved or froze to death. Those that did not die of starvation were often taken on long walks and simply shot and buried in ravines.

The pictures of the liberation of the concentration camp by the American soldiers were exceptionally moving. They showed skeletons of men reaching out through the fence as the US soldiers approached. Other pictures captured rail cars full of hundreds of deceased prisoners who had died inside the rail car on their way to the camp.

Just days before being captured by the Americans, the guards had taken thousands of prisoners on a death march through the mountains with little food or water and shot the majority who simply could not walk anymore. The cruelty was beyond anyone's comprehension.

Neither Blair nor I talked as we hitched back to the city. Our ride, a young German, knowing where we had just been, also never said a word.

We did find out later that day that the presentation centre was only built under significant pressure from the relatives of those who died there. The relatives wanted to show the citizens of Germany what had happened just twenty years prior.

It was so hard to rationalize this barbarous time in German history with the Germany of the present day. What a contrast between those singing in the Munich beer halls with those who lost their lives in a concentration camp just a few kilometers away.

We spent the rest of the day in the old town and later in the evening found ourselves at the Hofbräuhaus for our last night.

In Athens, we had decided that we should both have about ten dollars in our pocket when we arrived in New York for our hitchhike home. As the night wore on in Munich and Blair and I began to run out of money, we made a stupid decision to reduce that amount of money for North America to just eight dollars each, then five dollars, and spend the extra money on a final dinner on our last night in Europe.

I wanted to bring home a distinctive Hofbräuhaus mug and had twice been caught by guards as I tried to smuggle one out. But one of the California girls I had met earlier told me she would smuggle a mug out for me. As we left as a group, I watched her simply place the mug between her legs underneath her short skirt and waddle past the guards at the door.

That mug sits in my office today.

We hitched to Luxembourg with no hassles. The next day, we made our final hitch from the youth hostel to the airport, a distance of only seven kilometres. Not knowing the drill, we arrived a good four hours before the plane left and checked in well before the other passengers arrived.

We were going home after an incredible adventure. To say both Blair and I had changed would be a massive understatement. We had learned to survive on nothing, adapt to circumstances and come out ahead. We were both far more confident in our ability to handle situations.

Yet, being small-town guys, neither Blair nor I had ever been on a plane before. I was nervous, sure that the altitude problem and my vertigo would creep up and get me in spades. I feared I would be dizzy the entire trip, yet had no choice but to get on the plane, close my eyes and hope.

Blair took the window seat, which was great for me and great for him. We were heading for Iceland, where we would refuel, and would land fourteen hours later in New York at what is now called JFK airport.

Looking out the window, Blair was giving me a blow-by-blow description of what was happening as we sat on the tarmac. I noticed the pilot seemed to be having trouble starting the plane. I had no idea if this was a normal part of the process or if something was amiss. Blair got a bit excited as someone put a ladder up against the wing and was climbing up to investigate something. This was disconcerting, to say the least. After a few minutes, the guy came down to the ground and we could hear the sound of the plane running smoothly. In no time at all, we were out on the runway, then going full blast into the air. Blair continued to give me a play-by-play, as I had my eyes nowhere near that window.

I was thrilled with the ride. There was really no indication that we were flying. It almost seemed fake. Were we really off the ground? In only one day, we were now doing what had taken eight days for us on the way over: crossing the Atlantic Ocean. Like our ship on the way over, apparently Icelandic Airlines was the slowest way you could go by air from Europe to North America, but we didn't care.

On arrival at the airport in New York, reality set in. Blair and I had just one ten-dollar traveller's cheque between the two of us: exactly five dollars each to get from New York to home, some four thousand kilometres away. I blame this on the power of the beer at the Hofbräuhaus. We cashed the cheque at the airport, grabbed our packs and headed for the road. Not knowing what exact route would take us out of New York on the way to Chicago, we got out on the road where the taxis were arriving and started hitchhiking in a westerly direction.

Our first ride let us off on the freeway at the last turnoff before the entrance to the Lincoln Tunnel, which we knew was the right direction. We hopped over the barriers and hitched a ride at a pullover area directly in front of the tunnel. A car stopped quickly. We were on our way through the tunnel and off on a route that led to Chicago and home.

Hitching entirely through the US was a shorter route home than the Trans-Canada. We would head north to Canada when we got to Idaho or Washington state. For most of the trip, we would hitch together, then on the last day, leave each other to head north to our parents' homes through two different border crossings. While we'd been gone, Blair's parents had moved to Cranbrook, a few hundred miles east of Kelowna but still in British Columbia.

There wasn't much to our cross-continental trip. We stopped just once. One of us would always sleep in the car while the other kept up the mandatory conversations with our driver. Besides, we didn't feel it was safe enough for both of us to fall asleep at the same time. After months of hitching, all our senses were on alert.

Our one stop was somewhere east of Chicago. We started to hit farmland and got out of our ride in the middle of nowhere. But just off the road was a large empty barn. Since it was soon to be dark and we were exhausted, we snuck in, jumped into our sleeping bags and slept for about ten hours.

Our hitch across the entire United States took us just over four days. A fork in the road in Idaho took me west for another two hundred miles and Blair north. We shook hands, hugged and said our goodbyes, having hitched almost three thousand miles in what must have been a record time.

It was late afternoon when I got my last ride and was dropped off only four or five blocks from my home. I half-ran and half-walked those five blocks in less than three minutes, eager to be home and see my mother and father. I can still see myself walking up the back stairs of our home and looking through the window in the door. There was my mother, as usual, cooking an

Probably the last shot of me hitching home somewhere in Idaho.
Notice the patches on the pack from various countries.
Blair and I were still friends after such a long time together.

early supper, as she called it, in the kitchen. We had both written a letter to our parents on the plane that we would probably be home in six days — tomorrow — and had mailed it at the airport. I had mentioned there was a remote chance I would be a day early or a day late but not to worry. I was sure she was expecting me the next day.

I can still see my mother's face, crying as she rushed to the door to hug me as I appeared out of nowhere. I had never seen her as happy and relieved. Even my father was overwhelmed that I was now back alive with no visible knife marks. I was exhausted. I looked in my pockets and found that I still had 45¢ left from my original stash of $380.

My mother looked at me. After a few minutes, she said, "Jimmy, don't ever do this again."

Acknowledgements

First, I must acknowledge my mother, Mary Kerr, who kept every letter I wrote from our trip. Reading those letters again, so many years after they were written, made me realize I needed to document the adventures and experiences of such an important period of my life.

My wife, Kelly, kept me focused for the two years it took to write this book. She was always supportive and dealt with my many ups and downs as I struggled with technology and describing my voyage in the written word. No one was happier that the book was finished than Kelly, and I am eternally grateful for her undying support.

To Blair, my travel mate and best friend, what can I say? Without Blair there would be no book. I would not have left Kelowna on my own. Thanks for all your support and encouragement and for being such a good friend over the last sixty years.

Other sources of inspiration were my good friends Garry Reynolds, Tracey Ball, and Larry and Alice Laberge. Together they urged me to get these stories down in print before it was too late. I am sure they all secretly hoped that once in print I would stop telling these stories again and again. I would like to thank Garry in particular, who was the first to look at a rough draft. With his eye for detail, he provided me with invaluable advice and prompted many changes to content and sentence structure.

To Heather Conn, a professional editor, a huge thank you. I found Heather through a search of local editors and could not have been more pleased with the constructive criticism she gave me. Her focus was encouraging me to provide far more detail about the places we visited and to add dialogue wherever I could, all the while not changing my choppy style of writing. She vastly improved the book.

To Jo Blackmore and all her staff at Granville Island Publishing, another monster thank you. Jo's approach was tailor-made to my requirements. She was able to steer me through the many steps required to have the book professionally published. Her calm manner, depth of knowledge and years of experience made all the choices easy by convincing me she was right, not a simple task at times.

Jo assigned the book to one of her editors, Edward Zegarra. Ed offered numerous excellent ideas to improve the book. He emphasized the need for even more detail about the events and the cultural atmosphere of the places we visited, often from a historical point of view. Further, he emphasized the need to develop more of Blair's personality and to integrate the dynamics between the two of us into the storyline. Ed's advice was invaluable and I tried to incorporate into the book as many of his suggestions as I could.

The final step in the editing process was the copy edit. Jo's associate Marianne Ward was tasked with the difficult job of correcting my English and sentence structure. Thanks, Marianne, for picking up all those little errors and making the book more readable.

Jo's designer, Omar Gallegos, designed a wonderful cover for the book, picking up on the hitchhiking theme. As well, he transformed my Word document into a very professional-looking book. Taking thirty slides taken fifty-seven years ago, he and my brother-in-law, Mark English, made them look like they were taken yesterday. Thanks, Omar. The cover is outstanding and the photos are a great addition to the book.

The route we followed in Europe, North Africa and the Middle East is hard to follow without a few maps. I must thank Jamie Fisher for her patience in drawing the five maps for the book. I think they really help a reader understand just exactly where we went.

Last, I would like to thank my three girls, Brenda, Jennifer and Katharine, who all encouraged me to write this book. I hope this book inspires them to do everything they ever want to do in life.

Fun Facts

DAYS TRAVELLED AND EXPENSES

- Kelowna departure date: June 26, 1964
- Kelowna return date: March 17, 1965
- Days travelled: 264

AMOUNT SPENT

- Started with $380.00
- Earned in Montreal: $1.00
- Earned in Oslo: $65.00
- Payment from accident: $20.00
- Profit on selling Saab: $50.00
- Selling blood in Beirut: $18.00
- Selling blood in Athens: $10.00
- Total: $544.00
- Less amount remaining upon return: $0.45
- Total spent: $543.55
- Amount lived on per day: $2.06

FREE ACCOMMODATIONS ALONG THE WAY

- Homes of long-lost cousins and uncles: 15
- Homes of pen pals: 16
- Jails: 7
- Moving cars: 6
- Stationary cars: 2
- Side of the road: 5
- Campsites: 5
- New-found friends: 6
- Orphanages: 1
- Power stations: 1
- Border guard huts: 2
- Schools: 1
- Bus: 1
- Spanish ultra-cheap resort: 5
- Boats and planes: 9
- Hostels or hotels: 182

WAIT TIMES, RIDES AND MORE

- Number of rides: 1,459
- Longest wait: 9 hours (Tunisia)
- Shortest wait: 1 minute (Algeria)
- Longest ride: 1,723 kilometres (Tunisia to Alexandria)
- Shortest ride: 1.5 kilometres (getting out of Paris)
- Best line of the trip: "It's the custom in Europe not to put your lights on at dusk." (Blair)
- Worst line of the trip: "Who's first?" (in our hotel room in Tunis)
- Funds on hand upon arrival back in New York: 5 bucks

- Estimated library fines owing for three books taken out from Marrakesh library in 1964: $12,483.30 (57 years × 365 days × 2¢ a day per book)
- Best price for selling two stolen blankets: equivalent of $3.00
- Number of litres of beer drunk for free on the Heineken Brewery tours: 26 (for two people)
- Height of Cheops pyramid in number of blocks: 220
- Number of blocks Jim climbed before he froze: 51

Jim Kerr was born in 1945 and was brought up in Kelowna, BC. He attended the University of British Columbia out of high school and dropped out after his first year to hitchhike through Europe and North Africa with his best friend, Blair Campbell.

Soon after, Jim returned to earn an arts degree in economics at UBC, after discovering his knack for quick calculations at currency-exchange booths over the course of his journey. He has lived in Vancouver, BC, ever since and enjoys golfing and travel during his retirement after a successful career as a partner in a national chartered accounting firm.

After many years boring his close friends and family with countless stories of his epic voyage, he committed to writing *Meet Me in Cairo* at their behest. Jim is married to his wife, Kelly, and has three daughters and one son. He currently spends a quarter of the year travelling around the world, often arranging adventure bike tours with friends to far-flung places such as Chile and Myanmar.

www.meetmeincairo.ca